Bunny Williams' POINT OF VIEW

Three Decades of Decorating Elegant and Comfortable Houses

Bunny Williams'
POINT OF VIEW

Three Decades of Decorating Elegant and Comfortable Houses

WRITTEN WITH DAN SHAW
PRINCIPAL PHOTOGRAPHY BY FRITZ VON DER SCHULENBURG
BOOK DESIGN BY DOUG TURSHEN, WITH DAVID HUANG

STEWART, TABORI & CHANG, NEW YORK

DEDICATION

This book is dedicated to all my wonderful clients. It is their enthusiasm, vision, taste, trust, and sense of humor that inspires me every day. Interior design is a collaborative effort and I have had the best partners. I can honestly say I have the best job in this world thanks to them.

To the amazing architects that I have had the pleasure of collaborating with on the many projects. Ferguson & Shamamian, Jeffery Smith, Ernesto Buch, John Murray, Nassar Nakib, Andy Giambertone, Tom Kirchhoff, Hottenroth & Joseph, David Ellison, and Gil Schafer.

To my office staff past and present. Without all of them—both designers and administrators—this body of work could never have been completed.

To Fritz von der Schulenburg for his amazing photographs, Doug Turshen for his exacting eye, and Dan Shaw for his magical pen. And to Leslie Stoker who has always given the best advice and supported our vision.

To the memory of my parents and, of course, to John.

CONTENTS

INTRODUCTION

It's a spring morning in Charlottesville, Virginia. A young girl opens the back door of a modest brick Georgian house, and she races across the lawn. She runs between the peony beds toward a large field, her dogs following close behind her. She heads toward the woods and a small, white clapboard playhouse in the corner of the garden. There is a Dutch door that opens into a tiny room (once upon a time it was the well house) with two wicker chairs and a battered green army trunk with dress-up clothes, assorted dolls, and stuffed animals. There is a knee-high table with a miniature tea set, where she gives parties attended by the dogs, the dolls, a favorite stuffed bear, and Libby Palmer, her best childhood friend. Behind the house, there is a field covered with what seems like a million naturalized daffodils, which bloom under ancient apple trees. The young girl spends hours playing dress up, picking daffodils, and hosting tea parties for imaginary friends. She is never bored, because there are endless ways to arrange and rearrange her favorite things.

This was my first house. Although it was only about eight square feet, it was a huge source of happiness. As a child, I had no idea that I would become an interior designer. But looking back, it is clear that I've always loved playing house.

We lived on a small farm on Garth Road in Charlottesville, whose architecture was influenced by Thomas Jefferson and his designs for the University of Virginia. There was my mother, father, and older brother, Jimmy, along with assorted horses, ponies, cows, chickens, and lots and lots of dogs, as my father raised beagles. There was a small formal garden with boxwood and roses and a large vegetable garden, where we grew tomatoes, corn, okra, peas, and lettuce. The front walk was lined with boxwood. *Magnolia grandiflora* provided cuttings for the house in all seasons. We used the leaves to make Christmas wreaths and floated the lovely, porcelain white blooms in silver bowls on the dining table for special parties.

My mother loved her home. She not only had an innate sense of style when it came to decorating, but also took a hands-on approach to every aspect of homemaking. The fig jam we had for breakfast had been put up in her kitchen. With help from our housekeeper, Mrs. McAlister, she canned the tomatoes and okra and froze the corn and beans that we ate all winter. I remember accompanying my mother to visit the Curtain Lady, as we called her, as they worked out the design for a ruffled chintz valance for a bedroom window. I recall going to a country auction with both of my parents where they bid on the large rectangular, bleached-pine table that ended up in front of the picture window in the living room. At Christmas, we made wreaths from nuts and beads, and felt ornaments in the shape of animals to be sold at the church fair. When I wasn't playing outside, I was inside working on a project, whether it was baking cookies or knitting a scarf for Daddy's birthday (I shudder to think of how many of these he got!).

Our house was designed by Tommy Craven, an architect friend of my parents' who understood how they wanted to live. The brick exterior was painted a soft yellow with contrasting black-green shutters. The entrance hall had an antique red-backed Heriz carpet that I still have. To the left, you entered into the living room, which had a fireplace on the long wall and windows on each end. The large window at the far end looked toward the Blue Ridge Mountains; it was an idyllic, unforgettable view. The living room rug was made for Mother in North Carolina, and it was a rosy red and off-white plaid, which was quite avant garde for the time. Most people we knew had Oriental carpets in their main rooms. The walls were painted a flat, dark green, and the furniture was slipcovered in a mellow printed cotton. There were bookcases built along the wall opposite the fireplace, which held volumes of literature and poetry, and picture books on antiques and gardens, along with my mother's collection of English porcelain. The dining room had an American faded mahogany table with stenciled black painted chairs. To this day, I love the combination of a wood table with painted chairs. There was an early pine corner cabinet with a pedimented top that held a blue-and-silver lusterware tea service, which I inherited and often use for afternoon tea. Off the living room was the covered porch with an outdoor fireplace. In the summer, there was a canopy of heavenly blue morning glories, a flower that is still one of my favorites. There was a small study and a large screened-in porch off the kitchen where we ate most of our summer meals.

As we were related by marriage to the Garths (the namesake of our road and a prominent local family), many cousins lived nearby. Aunt Berta was the matriarch of the family. She lived in a rambling nineteenth-century farmhouse on hundreds of acres. We had Sunday lunch at her home almost every week with various relatives—from babies to octogenarians. It was the warmest and most welcoming house in town. The large living room had an impressive faded Oriental rug and the very comfortable furniture was slipcovered in a cheerful red-and-white toile. There was enough seating for the entire extended family. The room was filled with gleaming silver trophies won at various equestrian events, and the walls were hung with many paintings of the famous horses that Aunt Berta's family had owned.

My favorite place was the sun porch with its big cherry red leather sofas and chairs. One wall was covered from floor to ceiling with framed eight-by-ten, black-and-white photographs of every member of the family at various moments in their lives. The pictures were hung close together, as if a metaphor for what a tight-knit family we were. The photographs were a constant source of entertainment as they would inspire the elders to tell funny stories about each other.

Meals at Aunt Berta's were extraordinarily delicious because everything came from her land. Short beaten biscuits were served with roasted quail and a slice of country ham that had been cured in the smokehouse. The adults sat at the long English Victorian mahogany table in the dining room that was covered with a pristine white linen cloth. The children dined at a table in the breakfast room. I am fairly certain it wasn't until I was a teenager that I got to sit at the Big Table.

One of the most memorable things about Aunt Berta's house was that it was perpetually ready for company. People would just drop in around 5 o'clock every day, and there was always a supply of ham biscuits, cheese straws, and thin, round tomato sandwiches ready for any guest. In the refrigerator, there was invariably a pitcher of very strong Bloody Marys, and the ice bucket in the living room was full of ice. Aunt Berta's style has had a profound effect on my life and career, and I strive to give all my clients homes that are as comfortable and welcoming as hers.

Aunt Berta's daughter and my godmother, Mary Porter (or Porte as we called her), lived on an adjacent property in a white-painted brick Georgian House with black shutters. The spacious entrance hall had a grandfather clock, and her powder-blue living room was quite formal with an elegant Aubusson carpet. The house was the scene of many cocktail buffets. I can still taste the crabmeat casserole and ham biscuits along with the many other tasty tidbits that were served from the dining room while guests of all ages wandered from room to room. Like my mother, Porte was always decorating some part of her house. When she entertained, the family silver was polished and the crystal was sparkling. Though her house was more formal than her mother's, it had the same gracious sensibility. Another wonderful cousin was Josephine, who had a house filled with beautiful painted Italian furniture This was quite a contrast to everyone else's English and American furniture, and I found it very exotic. Today, painted furniture with its mellow patina is one of my weaknesses. Josephine had unusual taste, which really opened my eyes to the rewards of being daring and individualistic.

From early on, I did not want to only play house. I wanted to make tangible things, and I loved to use my hands. I remember stringing wooden beads or making potholders from cotton rags. At school, art class excited me much more than algebra. I made a lot of pottery vases for my mother, who would use them for her flower arrangements. When I was fifteen, I was allowed to spend the summer in New York with my father, who had recently taken a job there. The plan was that while he was at the office, I would take art classes. On my own, I researched art schools and chose one located at Carnegie Hall merely because I had heard of Carnegie Hall. I enrolled in a beginner's drawing class and was told to return the next day with a pad of sketch paper and some charcoal. I wasn't nervous at all until I realized that I was at least fifteen years younger than anyone else in the class. Everyone took their regular places and the only empty seat was in the front of a small circle. I sat down by an easel, looking for the table that I expected would hold the bowl of fruit that we would draw. But there was nothing to look at. A few moments later, a large middle-aged woman in a robe entered the room and stood in front of the class. She dropped the robe and stood there stark naked, assuming a languid pose. I froze. I was horrified. All I could do was look down at my blank pad; I was so embarrassed to be in a co-ed class with a strange naked lady. The teacher approached me and asked if this was my first life drawing class. I whispered, "Yes," and she told me that this was the best way to learn to draw and encouraged me to start slowly and outline the form. I began hesitantly. By the end of the summer, I had learned how to *see*. I began to see relationships between forms, to pay attention to proportions, and to view a whole as the sum of its parts. To this day, I never look at a room, a piece of furniture, or a garden without mentally making a note of the relationship among the components.

Luckily, my father only asked if I liked my class and did not ask to see my drawings. When I returned home to Virginia, my mother did ask to see what I had done all summer. She was shocked that I had been drawing nudes but was impressed with my results. My Uncle Joe, who was an artist, congratulated me on my work and encouraged me to continue. He said that drawing from life was one of the best ways to train one's eye. I could not agree with him more.

I took another trip that same year that had a profound effect on my life. My parents and I went to stay at The Greenbrier in White Sulphur Springs, West Virginia. The hotel had been renovated and redecorated by the high society New York decorator Dorothy Draper, and it took my breath away. Having had a fairly conventional upbringing, I had never seen such things in my life: Black carpets with cabbage roses! Enormous neo-Baroque white-plaster framed mirrors! Technicolor chintzes and bold wallpapers! It was like the set for a grand opera. I just could not believe my eyes.

My parents knew the owners, so we got the V.I.P. tour and saw many suites and bedrooms. This is when I first understood the job of the interior designer. I thought, *What fun—somebody got to pick out all these things and chose all these colors!* I got the idea that it would be fun to be an interior designer myself.

When it was time to look at colleges, I knew I wanted to go someplace with an interior design program. I chose Garland Junior College, which was an all-women's school in Boston (it is now part of Simmons). I took art classes and worked at stores in Boston to gain exposure to the world of design. I suppose it really was a finishing school, but everything I learned there has been useful to my career. Indeed, the best part of our education was having to run the townhouses where we lived on Commonwealth Avenue. Every two weeks, a different group was in charge of the house. We had to plan the menus, order the food, and keep within a budget. We had to make sure the house was clean and orderly. I called it Vacuuming 101. It's too bad there aren't still courses in how to run a household because hardly anyone knows how to do it anymore.

When I was twenty, I moved on my own to New York City. I got an apartment on the East Side with an old friend from Charlottesville, and I went to work at Stair & Co., the best English antiques shop in the city. I was hired as a receptionist, which is what polite young ladies did back then. It turned out to be a fantastic job because my responsibilities included writing out descriptions for the tags for every shipment that came in and matching them up to the invoices. I learned how to identify Hepplewhite, Chippendale, and Adam furniture; to tell the difference between Staffordshire and Worcester porcelains; to appreciate the characteristics of mahogany, satin wood, and burled walnut. For two and a half years, I catalogued all these things, touching them and examining them closely. I got to understand the feel of really good china and appreciate the proportions of a really good chair.

I had no idea at the time how much I was learning. Now because of this training, I am able to go in and out of a junk shop in ten minutes and if there is anything good I will probably find it. (The only person I know who is better at finding treasures in junk shops is my husband, John.) My eye is trained so that I look beyond the junk. If it's bad, my mind doesn't even take it in. If there is something with good proportions or a pretty finish, my eye lands on it. People always ask me how I shop so fast and I explain that I only see what's good.

I decided I did not want to pursue a career as an antiques dealer or a shopkeeper. (Many, many years later, though, John and I did open a garden antiques shop, Treillage, on the Upper East Side). I wanted to be a decorator and I decided that I wanted to work for Mrs. Henry (Sister) Parish, who was arguably the best traditional decorator in the United States. I had been in homes Mrs. Parish had designed and I admired her style. (I am always amazed that people refer to her as Sister, because I worked with her for twenty-two years and always called her Mrs. Parish.) I was hired as an assistant to her partner, Albert Hadley, who has been called the Dean of American Decorating.

One day not long after I started at Parish-Hadley, I was asked to deliver some samples to an apartment on Fifth Avenue. I was always running errands, so I did not think much of it until I arrived at the front door of Mr. and Mrs. William Paley, who were probably the most admired and envied couple in the city at that time. He was the founder and chairman of CBS. She was a fashion icon and an extraordinary hostess. The butler opened the door, and my jaw dropped when I saw over his shoulder in the hallway Picasso's *Boy Leading a Horse*, which I had studied in school. It had never occurred to me that paintings like that were hanging in people's houses. The butler could tell that I was an appreciative audience, and he sweetly took me into the big taxi-cab yellow drawing room with its van Goghs, Coromandel screens, and Regence mirrors. I was amazed because I instantly felt that this room was as comfortable as it was grand. You wanted to come in, sit down, and light a cigarette. (In those days, there was a beautiful ashtray on every table.) Although the flower arrangements were the most sumptuous I had ever seen and every surface was gleaming and immaculate, it was not intimidating. It was cozy. The three furniture groups were arranged so the room was comfortable for two people having a private tête-à-tête or for a large cocktail party. Amidst all this elegance, Mrs. Parish and Mrs. Paley had decided to slipcover some Régence chairs in hand-blocked batik sarongs. I was only twenty-two when I saw this apartment and it made a lasting impression, for I now understood how comfort and chic could coexist.

I learned a lot from Mrs. Parish and Albert, who each had different strengths. Mrs. Parish was a master at furniture arrangement. She could put more furniture in a room than anyone I have ever seen. She was a completely instinctive designer. She couldn't explain anything. If she drew a floor plan, it was on the back of a napkin and everything was out of proportion. But she could buy furniture without measuring. I don't think she even knew how to open a measuring tape!

Albert was the opposite. He was the most extraordinary teacher. He taught me to use a scale ruler and read floor plans. Every day was a master class. Though Albert could create wonderful traditional rooms, he was a true modernist. His own rooms were well edited and special because of the way he would mix old and new things to create stunning combinations. He was always seeking out new artisans, new finishes, new lighting; he liked to make exciting spaces. All of us who worked under him also developed the discipline to organize and manage a complex project. His modest, gentlemanly manner set the highest standards for a work ethic.

You always learn from people with great taste. You learn from people who really know how to live, and living well takes effort. You have to have high expectations. I learned a lot from Parish-Hadley's clients such as Mrs. Paley, Mrs. Charles Engelhard, and Mrs. John Hay Whitney. Their houses were inspirational and magical, and I was lucky to be exposed to their great style. Mrs. Paley kept a photo album of her table settings so her staff could set the table exactly as she had done before. I thought that was a fabulous idea.

You learn a lot from people who really care about their houses. I remember going to Mrs. Whitney's country house, Greentree, and discovering that she had a greenhouse where she grew all the flowers for the house. What luxury! I recall visiting Mrs. Thomas Jefferson Coolidge outside Boston whose front hall was filled with pots of out-of-season blooming tulips that were exactly the right shade for the room. I thought that was the ultimate luxury! And yet it also provided a lesson in how even a little bit of live greenery can animate a room. When you add a beautiful bouquet of flowers or a scented candle, you see and smell a room come alive.

A beautiful, comfortable home can give you and your family a sense of security. If you make your home personal and meaningful, it becomes your haven. There is no better feeling than walking through your front door at the end of the day or after a long trip and being happy to be home.

For a breakfast room, I commissioned the late Robert Jackson to paint garden landscapes on the walls. The painted nineteenth-century French chairs are upholstered in blue leather.

I.
MY POINT
OF VIEW

*For a house on the beach, the circular
staircase was paneled in washed limed oak.
A hand-woven runner flows down the
stairs along with a hand-wrought iron railing.*

I T IS 10 A.M, AND MR. AND MRS. NEW CLIENT ARE scheduled for their first meeting in my East Side Manhattan office. After welcoming them and offering coffee or sparkling water, I show them around the loft space that I have made my home away from home by furnishing it with things I love such as a worn leather sofa with nailhead trim. I notice whether they comment on my bookcases, which are framed by wooden Corinthian columns that I found years ago at a Maine antiques shop; I am hoping to glean some insight into their taste. It's essential that my clients understand me as much as I need to understand them, because I will be helping them make very personal decisions, and we need to be comfortable, if not intimate, with each other.

My approach to decorating extends beyond my ability to design a floor plan, purchase antiques, and hire expert upholsterers, carpenters, and painters to execute my vision. What I design are backdrops for living. I want to create rooms to be used, not just showplaces to be admired. My office reflects my ethos, and I am always pleased when new clients get it. I remember my initial meeting with a wonderful lady from Tennessee, who became one of my favorite clients. She arrived with her architect, her landscape designer, and the project manager who would coordinate everything. After introductions and chitchat about her trip to New York and people we knew in common, we moved into the conference room where croissants, muffins, and various beverages were laid out on top of the bookcase along with plates, forks, and perfectly pressed linen napkins. As everyone

Here I am taking Charlie and Lucy, my beloved terrier-mix dogs, for a walk in the courtyard of my New York apartment building, which was built in 1929.

was taking their places around my large, leather-topped conference table, I excused myself to get something I'd forgotten in my adjacent office. I overheard the prospective client exclaim to the group, "I *know* I can work with her." I was pleased because I could tell she appreciated and respected the hospitality that everyone was shown. To my mind, good manners are as much a part of a well-lived life as a comfortable sofa or a beautiful antique rug.

Knowing what you value is essential when decorating. When you open a door into someone's home, you are walking into a physical manifestation of their personality. Ideally, the environment should fit them precisely like a couture suit. Before I can design a home that will be appropriate for my clients, I need to know everything about them: Do they watch TV in bed? Do they have formal dinner parties or do more relaxed entertaining? Do they have overnight guests? Rambunctious children or grandchildren? How many books do they own? How many pairs of shoes? Do they wear their shoes in the house or do they go barefoot? Do they have pets? Do they collect paintings, photographs, or porcelains? Do they plan to have a full-time housekeeper and other staff? How will the house be maintained? I need to know these things to create suitable spaces for entertaining, dining, working, and relaxing. I use this information to make decisions about floors, fabrics, electronics, and lighting.

But before we can talk about floor plans or colors, we have to explore the big picture. I need to understand how they see themselves and what they want their

The library/dining room in my New York apartment is painted a dusty green. A Chinese coffee table sits in front of an antique Knoll sofa. An assortment of chairs—Italian, French, Deco—completes the seating group. The painting is a copy of a Vuillard.

home to represent. Do they need a home office or will a desk in the master bedroom suffice? Do they plan to have eighteen people for Thanksgiving dinner? Cocktail parties for seventy-five? Do they want to invest in good antiques and paintings? How much can they realistically spend?

Answering these questions is not always easy. You need to be ruthlessly honest if you want to make a happy home, and a project is only a success if it fits the owners' actual lifestyle. Of course, the location of the house dictates how it will be used. Are people going to be traipsing through the kitchen in wet bathing suits or snowy boots? I don't approach a house in Colorado in the same manner as one in Florida. Coming home to an apartment building with a doorman is different than entering your house through the garage as is commonly done in the suburbs.

I take a virtual tour of every room in a house and imagine people watching television, reading, surfing the Internet, playing Scrabble, paying bills. I ask my clients how they want each room to feel: formal, relaxed, serene, cozy, cheerful?

To help understand my clients' tastes, I usually recommend that they make a scrapbook of visual ideas. I encourage them to bring pictures of houses that they may have fantasized about in magazines or books. I ask them to tell me about hotels, inns, and historic houses that they have admired. I often show them my scrapbooks, which are filled with pictures of places that have inspired me, trying to elicit reactions so I can understand their sensibilities. We look at pictures of my previous projects, which I keep in red leather albums on a bookcase in my reception room. I want to know what gets them excited. How else can I help them realize their dreams?

I enjoy working with clients who are eager to learn more about the decorative arts. I think almost anyone can develop their taste and improve their eye if they are motivated. I encourage clients to visit auction houses and study the auction catalogues. I urge them to go to antiques fairs and to tour the period rooms at the Metropolitan Museum of Art in New York or Winterthur, the great Delaware estate and museum that was once the home of Henry Francis du Pont.

If you are not visually oriented and you hire a decorator, then it is really important to find someone whose taste you respond to and rely on her judgment. During the process, your eyes will hopefully open, and you will see the world in a new way.

In the end, good taste or bad taste is in the eye of the beholder, and fortunately, the world is filled with all kinds of tastes and many points of view. This book is a compendium of my taste as filtered through the needs and wishes of my clients. Though the term "eclectic" is overused today, it describes my look, which incorporates beautiful objects and furnishings from different centuries and countries. Although I own many Victorian objects— including my collection of unusual needlework pictures—I could never live in a heavily decorated, period Victorian interior. While I surround myself with lovely things—painted Italian furniture, gleaming Georgian silver, polished mahogany tables, fine bone china—they never get in the way of living or make any room off limits to my beloved dogs, Lucy, Charlie, and Elizabeth. You should never feel intimidated by your possessions nor that any room in your home is so precious that it must be saved for special occasions. Every day of your life is special.

I hope you find inspiration in this book that will help you transform your home in big and small ways. I hope that my point of view will help you discover yours.

A large English mirror hangs over a leather sofa covered with pillows made from antique textiles in my Manhattan office. A pair of 1940s tables sits on a contemporary rug by Allegra Hicks. Italian metal sconces hang above framed watercolors from my collection.

II.
FLOOR PLANS

A long entrance hall was divided into three columned bays linked together by a strong parquet floor made of three woods. The coat closet at the far end is hidden behind mirrors and metal gates designed by Gilbert Poillerat. A pair of large marble urns and pedestals stands in the foreground.

R OOMS, LIKE PEOPLE, ARE MEANT TO be useful. I don't believe living rooms should be reserved for parties. I don't think dining rooms should be fallow except on holidays. Long before the term "multitasking" became a buzzword, I was designing living and dining rooms that served several functions. I'll put a desk, a phone, a TV, and a bar in the living room. (I like to have a drinks tray out in the open so guests feel free to help themselves.) I will put a sofa and bookshelves in a dining room so that it can double as a library.

As much as I believe that good rooms evolve and get better with age, they need a strong foundation, which is why I always start with the floor plan. The instinct to place all the furniture against the walls is one of the most common decorating missteps I see. The average person encircles a room with sofas and chairs without thinking twice about how people will relate to one another when they are sitting down. You shouldn't have to move the furniture to have a conversation nor shout across the room. If you have to move a chair to read in good light or clearly see the TV, then the chair is not where it belongs. A chair placed by itself in a corner to fill up space will never be used.

You should not make any decorating decisions until you know how you are going to place furniture in a room. You should not go shopping until you understand

There are two distinct seating groups in this large country-house living room. The coffered ceiling has painted panels. The antique rug is nineteenth-century Persian.

how deep the sofa in the living room can be and how many side tables and armchairs can be accommodated. If you have heirlooms that you want to use, you'll have to tailor your plans to integrate them. Many of the most innovative floor plans are based on a single antique that has a domino effect on the size, scale, and placement of the other furniture to be purchased.

You can't look at sofas, tables, and chairs in isolation; you have to look at them in relation to all the other furniture in the room if you are going to create spaces that are balanced, nuanced, and harmonious. A common mistake many people make when they are starting out is to go into a store and buy the most comfortable sofa, which becomes the elephant in the room after it's delivered. If it's too long or deep, all the proportions of the room will be wrong. The room will be uncomfortable—aesthetically and emotionally. You have to be careful of overblown, upholstered furniture. I have most of my sofas custom-made so that they are exactly the shape and size I want. They must always be long enough so I can lie down and take a nap. That is non-negotiable. I always have my clients not only sit in a sofa but also stretch out on it before making a selection.

It is important to really study an empty room, starting with how you enter it and how you move through it if it leads to another room. Pay attention to the proportions, especially the height of the ceiling. If there is a low ceiling, consider adding a really tall piece of furniture to draw your eye upward. Is there a focal point, such as a fireplace or a large window with an amazing view? Where does the natural light come from and what time of day does it filter in? Are there floor or wall registers that cannot be covered? Is there any unnecessary opening that could be changed to create better wall space?

When thinking about the placement of furniture, you not only have to think about the floor plan but the elevations of the rooms. After moving pieces of furniture around on paper and designing seating groups as seen from above, I then study how the scheme will look in elevation against the walls and in front of the windows. Thinking three-dimensionally is the hardest thing to do, and you learn by studying well-done rooms. Anyone who cares about decorating ought to visit house museums and ancestral houses to see how the furniture is arranged (see Resources for a list of historic houses you can visit in the United States). Whenever I tour old houses in England and France, the first thing I notice is the furniture placement. I study the floor plan and make a mental note of what works and what does not. When looking at pictures of rooms in books, I will sometimes sketch out an interesting floor plan on paper.

To come up with the right floor plan, you need to spend time in each room and think about what you want to do there and what type of furniture is required. Where will you put your feet up and your coffee cup down? Imagine yourself in this room after work in the evening or on a lazy Sunday morning. Do you see yourself reading or watching television, writing thank-you notes or e-mailing, eating a sandwich, or playing cards?

I learned about floor plans from two experts: Sister Parish and Albert Hadley, who had completely different approaches even though they were business partners. No one could arrange furniture better than Mrs. Parish. For most people, it was too much furniture, but, after seeing how her living rooms worked for parties, I realized the need for several seating groups, small tables for cocktails, and a variety of lighting sources. Albert, on the other hand, was more of a minimalist and modernist. His own rooms always had a spare, sculptural quality, but as he entertained mostly large groups for cocktails, his schemes worked perfectly for him because his guests rarely sat down.

All rooms have daytime and evening personalities, and you must take both into account. During the day, when sun is pouring in, we gravitate to the windows, but in the evening these windows can be ominous black holes, reflecting the lights inside. If you live in a place where the exterior is illuminated at night—such as a big city or a hillside overlooking a town with twinkling lights—you may have a fabulous evening view. But most rooms do not have this and we want to turn away from the windows when the sun goes down and draw the curtains and blinds (see Chapter IV). Traditionally, furniture was arranged in front of the fireplace since it was often the only source of heat. Today, this is not necessary, so your floors plans can be more flexible and you don't have to organize a room around the fireplace. (By the way, consider converting your woodburning fireplaces to gas. Although I am a big fan of aromatic wood fires, they can be a real chore to stoke and the newer gas logs look more realistic than ever and provide a wonderful ambience at a flick of a switch. At my house in Connecticut, I burn real wood in my library for the smell and crackle, but I have gas logs in my kitchen, dining, and living rooms so I can have all the fireplaces going at once.)

Most rooms have a traffic pattern that you must study and consider before making a floor plan. Where are the doors and do they swing in or out? Is the room a dead end or does it lead to another? Does it open onto the garden? Study each wall elevation. Is the placement of windows and doors balanced or will you use furniture to compensate for structural flaws? I do not think all elevations need to be perfectly symmetrical, but there must be equilibrium: In my living room in the country, I have a fireplace in the center of a wall with a door to the library to the right of it, so on the left side I placed a tall eighteenth-century Swedish secretary desk for balance.

I think of doorways as large picture frames. When I stand on the outside looking into a room, I want to be lured into the space. What is the view framed by the portal? Is it a window, a view to another room beyond, or a wall? If it is a wall, then it needs a focus: a piece of furniture with a painting or mirror above it or a pedestal with a piece of sculpture. The trick is to create a vignette that looks as good from outside the room as within it.

Now come into the room. Where will you and your friends and family sit? I prefer furniture groups that accommodate at least eight people. In very large living rooms, I might have two or three seating areas with no fewer than six places to sit in each one. This usually means a sofa, four armchairs, and two benches, or a pair of sofas and several chairs. I have found that rarely do more than two people sit on a sofa unless it is a very long banquette or an L-shaped seating unit. If the room has a fireplace centered on a long wall, you can place a sofa opposite and put the chairs on each side and the benches in front of the fireplace. If there is no fireplace, the furniture group can float in the center of the room. I then might use a long table with a painting over it as the focal point on an extended wall. For an apartment in Florida that had a very large living room with views on two adjacent walls, I decided to place a large furniture group in the center of the room. A pair of sofas faced each other with a coffee table in between. A third sofa with a different silhouette faced a pair of large French bergeres. On the long wall opposite a wall of windows, I put a long bookcase with cabinets for storing games and puzzles. As these clients were great card players, we put two card tables in opposite corners, and they can also be used for afternoon tea or a casual supper.

I also like to use furniture of different heights in a room. It is important to have a tall piece of furniture to carry your eye up to accentuate the height of a room. This can also be accomplished with a tall mirror or painting. I like to use tables of different heights, too. A table 30 inches high works well next to a sofa, as it puts an average-sized lamp at the correct height when you are seated. I like the bottom of the lampshade to be at eye level when you are seated. If you have a lower side table that's 24 or 26 inches, then you have to find a much taller lamp. I like very low tables next to a chair as a place to rest a glass of wine or cup of tea; without them, entertaining becomes very awkward.

When using matching pairs in a room, I try to vary the arrangement a bit. For example, if I have a pair of chairs next to a sofa, I would probably not use a pair of tables and put a pair of lamps on them. You can have symmetry without relying on pairs which can get boring.

When it comes to bedrooms, size really dictates what you can do. A comfortable mattress is more important than anything, and that is a very personal decision. The best size to my mind is a California King, which is narrower (72 inches) and longer (84 inches) than a traditional king-size bed. I think king-size beds are terribly proportioned—they're too boxy. And now, finally, it is easy to get wonderful sheets for California Kings. A queen-size bed is a lovely shape, but it is not large enough for some couples, especially if there are frequent visits from children or dogs.

If your room is large enough, you may want your bedroom to double as a sitting room. I live in my bedroom in the city, which has bookcases, a television, a dressing table, a chair, and ottoman. I have a canopy bed, which I consider cozy. Some people find them claustrophobic. They are wonderful in rooms with high ceilings, and, ironically, they are even better in rooms with low ceilings because they make the ceilings look taller. Nothing's more dramatic than a tall bed in the middle of a room.

If you take the time to plan your rooms, you are apt to make the right choices. Resist the urge to be impulsive. Keep in mind the carpenter's adage: "Measure twice, cut once."

Both furniture groups in this living room have painted Continental furniture. A large painted Italian panel hangs over a Swedish sofa. A pair of nineteenth-century French chairs pulls up to a large modern ottoman covered in antique fabric.

In a traditional library with contemporary art, a pair of Deco rosewood chairs faces an Anglo Indian coffee table. The sofa is flanked by square tables draped in felt. An eighteenth-century French slipper chair completes the seating group.

ABOVE: A seating group by the window in a corner of a large living room includes a curved sofa, a French gilt armchair, and a leather slipper chair from the 1940s. RIGHT: Antique chairs surround a modern dining table. The metal chandelier is 1940s. The niches hold marble busts representing the Four Continents, which was how the world was viewed in the sixteenth-century.

OVERLEAF: In the living room of my New York apartment, an English Regency sofa sits in front of a sunny window. The seating group around the fireplace includes a sofa and a pair of Swedish Klismos chairs that flanks a Chinese coffee table. A French desk stocked with stationery is in the foreground.

ABOVE: *An antique Italian desk sits in front of a window in an oak-paneled library. The chair with its original needlepoint upholstery faces the view.* RIGHT: *Modern uphol- stered pieces are mixed with antique chairs on a sunny glassed-in porch.*

III.
FLOORS, WALLS,
AND CEILINGS

This entrance hall was given special treatment with a complex parquet floor and stencil patterns painted on the plaster coffered ceiling. A pair of English library tables floats in the center with English Regency bookcases placed against the walls. Floor outlets were specified on the floor plan so the lamps could be inconspicuously plugged in beneath the tables.

I DECORATE ROOMS FROM THE BOTTOM UP, SO I always begin with the floors. It's a mistake to think you must live with the floors that come with your house or apartment. Floors have a profound effect on the ambience of a home. If they are not beautiful, there are many ways to make them special.

The floor in the entrance hall is especially important, and it should relate to the material of the house. As entrance halls are usually sparsely furnished, the floor becomes the focal point. I believe stone, brick, or stucco houses should have hard surface floors of marble, terrazzo, or terra-cotta tiles. Wood houses should have wood floors. The luster and finish of a floor gives character to a space. The smell and patina of freshly waxed wood floors, whether they are simple wide boards or an elaborate parquet pattern, set a definite mood. Hand-scraped wood floors (especially if they creak underfoot) give a feeling of warmth and age. Highly polished floors feel more formal and can look wonderful in modern houses as well as traditional residences.

There are so many ways to approach wood floors. A parquet floor made of different species of wood such as oak, walnut, and ebony can be an elegant, graphic treatment for a foyer. With simple, existing board floors, I often overlay a stenciled pattern that adds visual excitement. I am also particularly fond of painted wood floors. For one formal Georgian house in Connecticut, I painted the wood floors to simulate squares of marble. The sound and feel of walking on the wood is softer than walking on stone, but the faux marble gives a hall a dignified elegance

In a stucco house, an antique stone floor imported from Portugal sets the tone for the entrance hall and echoes the stone door trim.

that's not as grand as genuine polished marble would be. In warmer climates, painted wood floors provide a light, cool sensibility. Stenciling and paint can often transform a bad wood floor into something special.

As for stone floors, I prefer a honed finish to a highly polished surface. Antique stone floors always seem warmer than new ones. When it comes to terra-cotta floors, I'm of two minds: I like like them highly waxed or left natural for a rustic feeling, depending on the mood of the house.

For the main rooms of a house, I prefer monochromatic floors because they will undoubtedly be covered by area rugs with a pattern. When a room is filled with furniture, rugs, and art, plain floors are the prudent choice. If you will be installing new floors, choose your wood carefully. My favorite is walnut: When it's highly polished, walnut has tremendous character and warmth. When properly finished, walnut becomes the color of rich honey. Walnut and mahogany have the most beautiful grain. Chestnut can have a more rustic complexion, for it has much more texture. White oak floors are versatile, and they can be stained very dark for a dramatic look, or bleached and pickled with white paint so they're the color of a sandy beach. Avoid less expensive red oak, which is hard to stain a beautiful color. I love old pine floors, but I have found that new pine can have too much red and yellow in it for my taste. For the house we recently built in the Dominican Republic, I chose wideboard Honduran mahogany. It was easy and convenient to import, and the wide boards have the most beautiful grain. We finished it with a satiny polyurethane that enhances the cognac color of the wood.

RUGS

Before selecting paint colors and fabrics for a room, I choose the rug. I prefer rugs with all over pattern and softer colors so the carpet will lie on the floor—I don't want a rug to jump out at me. I want it to be a backdrop for art and furniture. Agras, which come from north central India, are my favorite because of their sophisticated designs and subtle coloring. I also love Sultanabads, which were made in Persia in the late nineteenth century for the European market, because of their overall designs; Oushaks from Turkey because of their summery pastel colors; Persian Tabriz rugs that often have a field of stems, fronds, and leaves; flat woven Indian dhurries for their informal quality; and Bessarabians, which are flat woven carpets with bright nineteenth-century floral patterns. Needlepoint carpets are wonderful for bedrooms, but be careful where you put them because they are very fragile. I like bold carpets in dining rooms because there is less fabric to compete with, and much of the rug is covered by the table. Still, you should not use a flat weave carpet in the dining room because the pulling and pushing of chairs will eventually do damage

When I do not want a lot of pattern on the floor, I always use sisal or sea grass rugs. Sometimes when the floors are really terrible, I install wall-to-wall sisal and use small area rugs on top. For bedrooms and studies, I like to use hand-woven cotton and linen rugs that have wonderful texture and subtle patterns.

This library's coffered ceiling was made of the same butternut as the paneled walls. A blue striped linen-and-silk fabric covers the plaster walls, picking up the color from the antique Sultanabad rug.

Although I am partial to antique rugs, there are many wonderful copies of Oriental rugs on the market today. I favor flat, thin carpets over thick ones. My preference is as much aesthetic as practical: It is easier to pull a chair up to a desk or dining table on a flat rug, and they are easier to walk on, too.

As for what size rug you need, I always scale in a rug on my floor plan before I go shopping. In a smaller room, I want a rug big enough so that all the furniture will sit on the carpet. I don't want the border of floor showing to be more than twelve inches. A small rug in a small room will make the room seem smaller, because you'll focus on the size of the rug. In a larger room, you can have more than one rug but it must fit the furniture groups. I find lots of little rugs in a room to be confusing.

WALLS

In most new construction, there are vast expanses of banal Sheetrock walls that need to be covered. For simple walls, I use paints by Farrow & Ball, a British firm that uses traditional formulations, or those by Donald Kaufman, the expert New York colorist. Both companies' paints have a rich depth of color, which changes with the light. For a New York apartment where I wanted a soft white room, I consulted personally with Kaufman, who is a genius when it comes to mixing pigments. The color he made for me had the depth of real ivory; though the room was basically white, the walls were warm and alive. For the entrance hall of a five-story townhouse, I wanted a color that was like the inside of a ripe peach. The walls are dynamic because the color changes depending on the light. During the day, it reads very yellow but at night, with the light from the sconces and lamps with cream silk shades, it's an intoxicating orange.

Another way to imbue walls with rich color is to use a wash or glaze over a solid color. A white wall can be glazed with a thin coat of color that gives the walls texture and depth. I prefer very simple striated glazes that are very fine, or a glaze applied with a brush that is gone over with cheese cloth or a stipple brush. I do not think glazes should be too pronounced or wild.

Nothing is better than plaster walls. If you have Sheetrock walls, you can run a skimcoat of plaster over them and the room will feel like it was plastered. You get a wonderful matte, chalky finish. If you tint the plaster with a color before applying it, you won't have to paint on top of it. The skimcoat will give your walls the hand-troweled look of an older house. I use different paint finishes—flat, eggshell, semi-gloss, high-gloss—depending on the circumstances. For a room flooded with daylight, I usually specify paints with an eggshell finish. Flat walls absorb light whereas shiny walls reflect it. In my New York apartment, which has a rather dark living room, I wanted to brighten the space, so the walls are done in an off-white Venetian plaster the color of an eggshell and then waxed so the light will bounce off the walls.

If the living room and entrance halls have plain painted walls, I might choose patterned walls for the dining room—a beautiful antique Chinese wallpaper or a custom hand-painted mural can be magical. Dining rooms can have more pizzazz than other spaces because you're in them for short bursts of time so they don't become overwhelming. Now that there are manufacturers reproducing the great Chinese wallpapers, I prefer to hire muralists to create one-of-a-kind scenes. Hiring decorative painters to create custom murals is a great American tradition. In the eighteenth and nineteenth centuries, itinerant painters traveled the country, offering their services door to door. (One of the best was Rufus Porter, who travelled around New England in the nineteenth century painting scenic murals.)

If you want patterned walls, you can always use fabric, which is warmer than paint or plaster. You can have the walls upholstered or

The walls of a sunny garden room are covered in a wooden lattice that is painted an ethereal gray-blue. The circles above the doors are fitted with antique mirrored panels.

you can have the fabric "paper-backed" so it can be hung like wallpaper, though elegant fabrics must be treated like upholstery or draperies when hung on walls. An English printed cotton can cozy up a bedroom, and an elegant silk Damask or exquisite hand-blocked Fortuny fabric with flecks of gold can add glamour to the walls of a dining room. For an elegant and masculine bedroom, I once upholstered the walls in dark green wool coaching cloth and used a handblocked, printed cotton print for the curtains.

If you have a large house, it's fun to have a paneled room. Men seem to have an affinity for wood rooms. They are beautiful filled with books. And stained wooden bookshelves are more practical than painted shelves, which get beaten up every time you remove a volume and put it back. Woods that I find make beautiful paneled rooms are walnut, butternut, oak, and blended mahogany.

Almost any style house can have a paneled library. The carving and moldings can be French- or English-inspired depending on what is appropriate. For a modern house, I'll put leather inserts in the paneling. But it's not necessary to have raised panel molding. You can use veneers on a solid panel in a diamond pattern for a contemporary look, which can make the entire room feel like a single, well-crafted piece of furniture. And though I tend to imagine libraries as dark, introverted rooms—I'm a big fan of mossy green or red lacquered libraries for New York apartments—they can be light, bright spaces as well. For a client in Florida, I designed a library of polished cyprus, an indigenous wood that is the color of sand. Cyprus is used all the time in Florida and it is normally rough and pecky. I had the wood sanded and polished to a sheen, which brought out its greens and yellows, making it more elegant.

CEILINGS

I t's a shame that it's not very common to have painted ceilings in American houses. When I started visiting Europe, I began to really appreciate painted ceilings. But I had my epiphany when I visited the Medieval Royal Palace of Sintra in Portugal. One coffered ceiling was painted with magpies, which was the king's way of mocking his wife and her courtiers, whom he considered annoying chatterboxes. I was very amused. I realized that I could have fun with ceilings and that they need not be a big white void. I tend to embellish higher ceilings, and find that the coffered ceilings in the grand old Meisner houses in Florida demand decorative treatment.

You can have decorative ceilings in a more casual country house, too. You can do the ceiling in wood. I like using unsawed rough boards in a herringbone or diamond pattern and then painting them white. It's an especially effective way to give texture to a new house.

Every floor, wall, and ceiling is an opportunity to play with light, color, and texture. They may be the basics, but the bones of your house deserve special treatment.

An intricately patterned dining room ceiling of white washed oak is unexpected and breathtaking. The walls are a melon-tinted, waxed Venetian plaster. Painted wheelback chairs sit on a patterned straw rug.

*ABOVE: Oak beams enhance a tray-ceilinged library. The custom bookcases were inspired by
ones in the house of the great French decorator Madeleine Castaing.
RIGHT: Gold tea paper on the ceiling warms the high-ceilinged dining room and gives the
room a cozy glow. Russian chairs surround an English oak Arts and Crafts table lit by Japanese
porcelain lamps plugged into floor outlets. The lamps' cords run between the leaves of the table.*

ABOVE: *The paneled plaster walls are glazed in shades of yellow and cream in the entrance hall of a Georgian house.* RIGHT: *Plaster panels add dimension to an entrance hall with a limestone and honed black marble floor. A tapestry hangs on the large wall above the staircase.*

The original coffered ceiling panels were embellished with stencil patterns inspired by a ceiling I saw in Italy. A handmade Portuguese needlepoint carpet covers the floor.

Having purchased this set of Swedish dining chairs for a mountain house, I decided to commission a mural that evoked walls I'd seen in Swedish interiors. Robert Jackson painted the stylish scenes as well as the faux bois paneling.

ABOVE: *In a house designed by architect Jeff Smith, the intricately coffered living room ceiling was painted in shades of white and the limestone floor was covered with antique Oushak rugs.* RIGHT: *In the dining room, the walls are upholstered in lime-green Fortuny fabric that was chosen because that color is woven into the antique Indian carpet.*

LEFT: *Antique Venetian lanterns were turned into sconces for the stone walls of a stair hall. ABOVE: In a gallery with a Gothic vaulted plaster ceiling, the patterned floor was made of three different limestones.*

ABOVE: An eighteenth-century Regence gilt mirror hangs on a coral stone wall above a rare French console table. RIGHT: Hand-painted wallpaper by de Gournay adds interest and warmth to a hallway. The runner is a reproduction Bessarabian.

The color of the polished travertine floors is echoed in the hand-painted canvas on the dining room walls.

ABOVE: The exceptionally tall ceiling of the room was done in polished butternut boards and large hand-hewn beams. A plaid Portuguese needlepoint rug covers the floor.
RIGHT: The cypress ceiling on a loggia complements the casual rattan furnishings.

*A collection of blue-and-white Chinese plates surrounds a rare
eighteenth-century Italian mirror on natural plaster walls.
An ebonized Portuguese cabinet holds more of the collection.*

ABOVE: Polished butternut paneling creates a warm feeling in a library. A handwoven linen-and-hemp striped rug covers the floor. RIGHT: The moldings in this entrance hall are painted in faux marble to complement the walls, painted to simulate cordovan leather.

A collection of nineteenth-century watercolor designs for faience plates was pasted to the wall and shadow lines were added to create a trompe l'oeil effect. The lower half of the wall was painted with trompe l'oeil moldings and paneling.

Squares of antique leather were applied to the walls
with nailhead trim and surrounded by polished fruitwood paneling. A nineteenth-century French brass
clock hangs above a simple black marble mantel.

LEFT: *A wooden floor is painted in a diamond pattern over the straight floor boards. The architectural prints were first mounted on sheets of marbleized paper and then glued to the wall. ABOVE: A collection of marbleizing designs was framed and hung in an octagonal hall. The floor is covered in a modern circular carpet.*

IV.
WINDOWS

A valance is embellished with cotton fringe and wooden tassels.

A S I WRITE THIS, I AM SITTING
by the fireplace in the living room of my nineteenth-century Federal farmhouse in northwestern Connecticut. The room has four French doors that open onto a terrace and a screened-in porch. The windows are cased with period nineteenth-century reed trim with corner blocks. I have never had curtains or blinds on them. During the day, the sun pours in, and in the evening the watery antique glass panes reflect the flames from the fire. I don't need curtains for privacy because I'm in the country and nobody can look in. Nevertheless, most windows do require curtains, and making up one's mind about them can be bewildering, for there are so many variables and styles to consider. (Opting out as I did in Connecticut is only rarely the solution.)

You should take time to study the windows. Analyze each opening and then step back and see the windows in elevation. You need to understand their form and function. Do they dominate the walls? Are they handsome or do they need to be masked? Is there a view to be framed? Do you want to be able to modulate the natural light? Are the windows large simple openings? Are they balanced in the room or off center? Should the windows and doors be improved? If your house has ugly, aluminum sliders, think seriously about replacing them with wooden French doors. A traditional house always looks better with windows that have

Handsome arched French doors require a simple
window treatment—panels of sheer linen that hang
from hand-hammered metal poles.

divided lights. In a modern house, large single-pane windows are appropriate. Windows must suit the style of the house.

I always design curtains to respect the architecture. If you have a house with tall, narrow windows, it's an opportunity to use traditional curtain styles incorporating swags, jabots, or shaped valances. For inspiration, I often refer to old curtain pattern books or my own extensive picture file of curtain designs that I have assembled from books and magazines over the years. I always make sketches for each window treatment by drawing a scaled elevation of the wall with the window placement. This way I can really see how the curtains should hang in relationship to the wall, enhancing the window but not smothering it. Good curtains are like a well-tailored suit: They disguise bad proportions and create a flattering silhouette.

Proper curtains must be beautifully made. They should have a flannel inner lining so they hang in a soft way. If they don't, the curtains will lack body and hang limp like sheets on a clothesline on a windless day. Traditional curtains always had embroidery or decorative trim, and I embellish them whenever appropriate. One of my favorite sources for curtain ideas is costume exhibitions, where I study the details on men's jackets; the trims on Renaissance and eighteenth-century clothing were *amazing*. Once you start looking, you will no doubt find curtain inspiration in unexpected places, too.

I think curtains should always touch the ground. I can't stand curtains that miss the floor—it's like having your trousers too short. When I measure curtains, I always make them $1/4$ to $1/2$ inch longer than the distance from the rod to the floor. It makes them look softer and fuller. Some people like curtains billowing or puddling on the floor, but I think that look is very difficult to maintain. It's especially hard when you vacuum and then try to get them back in place.

I never want to see the commercial curtain hardware, so it is important to figure out how the curtains will close. The simplest way is a metal or wooden pole with rings attached to the curtains, which means the curtains must be closed by hand. Good curtain workrooms can insert a traverse rod in a wooden pole that will allow the curtains to be closed with a side cord. Curtain valances are also an easy way to hide the unattractive curtain hardware and are especially helpful if the curtains are to be managed electronically, which is increasingly common. Valances can be made from a hard material like buckram for a structural effect, or they can be softer and swagged. For a modern house with a wide window, I might make a simple architectural valance or soffit to hide the curtain track.

You must think about how your curtains look from the street, too. The lining that you see from the outside is very important. If you have a house with windows on either side of the front door, you want the lining of the curtains to match. You don't want green on one side and gold on the other. I usually try to select a lining that goes with all the fabrics, but if I can't find one that works universally, then I'll make the lining in an off-white or a small neutral pattern. The lining should be the same for every window across the whole front of the house. This rule applies to window shades in the bedrooms. Use identical shades for all the windows facing the street. I like old-fashioned two-inch-wide Venetian blinds because they work in almost every situation.

If you cannot have your curtains made by an accomplished workroom, then keep the design very simple. I don't think expensive curtains are a wise investment unless you plan to stay in your house for a very long time. It would be much better to put that money into a wonderful piece of furniture that you can have forever. Curtains made for individual windows are often hard to reuse (though they can always be recycled as decorative pillows).

It is very important that the curtains be in harmony with the architecture of the house. When specifying curtains for large windows in a modern house, I always keep them plain: panels of fabric on a simple metal pole the same color as the walls. Covering a big modern opening with fancy swags and fringe looks out of place. Even if you are decorating a modern house with antiques, you should keep the curtains clean and uncomplicated. You shouldn't have elaborate curtains in a simple room; it's like wearing a ballgown to the movies

Traditionally, windows were small to keep out the cold, and curtains were meant to cut down on drafts. I still believe that heavy or elaborate window treatments should only be used when they relate to the scale of a room and its sense of history. If you have a formal room with good furniture, then you can have curtains with swags, jabots, and fringe.

Curtains can be problem solvers too, when you have awkwardly shaped or spaced windows. If there is a big distance between the window and the ceiling, then you make the curtains tall by having a valance that hits the moldings, and cover the space between the valance and the top of the window with a shade. It creates the illusion of a long, lean window. In my low-ceilinged bedroom in Connecticut, I found nineteenth-century Regency valances which I placed right at the ceiling to make the room seem taller.

If windows have an odd placement in a room, it is best that the curtains are the same color as the walls so that they blend in and don't call attention to themselves. I also think very large windows across a wall should always have monochromatic curtains. Otherwise, when the curtains are closed, you will have a large expanse of distracting pattern. If you have very wide windows, it's not where you want to put a lot of pattern. If you have a room with single windows proportionately spaced, then you can have curtains made of patterned fabric. But the more pattern you put at the window, the busier the room gets. If the same pattern, such as a floral motif, is used on all four walls, the room will look better with matching curtains. I often do this for clients who want pretty, romantic bedrooms.

When a window has a spectacular view of the mountains or the ocean, curtains are often unnecessary. However, shades that can be tucked up into pockets over an architectural valance to filter strong light are a very good idea. In places with very bright sun, such as Florida and Texas, I often use solar shades that cut the glare but still allow you to see out the window.

Fabulous daytime views often disappear at night. The best solution is to do beautiful unlined curtains that just hang at the side of a window; you draw them in the evening to give a little bit of softness and warmth instead of staring at a cold, black expanse of glass. Or you can try to light the view out your window. At my first house in the country, there was a large window at one end of the kitchen that reflected the whole room back at night. Fortunately, there was a big white birch outside that I could light, and then I had a wonderful evening view, and I did not have to put up curtains.

Bedrooms usually require curtains or shades for privacy and light control. I love old-fashioned, two-inch wooden Venetian blinds on single windows, especially where there is a window reveal in which to hang the shade. When working on new house plans with an architect, I always study the window details and plan how the windows are going to be treated. I have spent too many hours trying to design curtains for awkward windows that open into a room that negate almost any window treatment. I wish all architects had to design window treatments for a week before being allowed to design windows. Palladian windows in a bedroom are a challenge when the clients require complete darkness to sleep. A pocket has to be built into the top of the window for a shade to cover the curve. These problems can be solved in the planning stage. Windows that are double hung and have at least a three-inch reveal can easily accommodate a simple shade.

I also love tiny wooden matchstick pull-up shades: They give a wonderful texture to the window. Tortoiseshell bamboo blinds can be very chic in a dark, cozy library. For the guest rooms at my house in Connecticut, I use dark green linen roller shades that pull down behind the curtain panels so my friends and family can sleep late—if the roosters don't wake them up first!

ABOVE: Blue silk curtains lined in tangerine cotton are held back from the windows with special sunflower tiebacks. RIGHT: Plaid taffeta curtains are tied back to frame the windows as well as an English Regency rosewood desk.

ABOVE: A bay window is treated with panels of rich hand-blocked fabric from Robert Kime that hang from simple poles. RIGHT: Some views should never be obstructed by window treatments. A late nineteenth-century Arts and Crafts desk offers a wonderful spot to gaze at the Rocky Mountains.

ABOVE: *The many windows of this hallway have curtains made of custom embroidered silk from Holland & Sherry. RIGHT: The curtains' embroidery is echoed in the carvings on an eighteenth-century gilded Georgian chair.*

ABOVE LEFT: For a guest bedroom, printed linen curtains have matching shirred valances with special wooden fringe. ABOVE RIGHT: A balloon shade fits elegantly into the deep window reveal of a paneled library in New York City. Antique needlepoint pillows soften a corner banquette. RIGHT: The cotton taffeta fabric is shirred on a gilded pole and the curtain panels are trimmed in a four-inch contrasting cuff, as are the attached valances.

ABOVE: *The windows of this enclosed sun porch are treated with monochromatic Roman shades the same color as the walls; when they're drawn, the room maintains its character.* RIGHT: *Tailored box-pleated valances and straight hanging curtains frame French doors in a library with an antique Oushak carpet.*

In a bedroom with walls covered in a printed cotton, the curtains are made from the same fabric but not in the same style. Pull-up balloon shades hang over the window seat. The floor-to-ceiling curtains have a matching shirred valance trimmed with bell fringe.

V.
FURNITURE

A 1950s lacquer screen stands behind a painted Venetian sofa. A nineteenth-century French chair is upholstered in linen embroidered with squiggles inspired by Matisse. A large, carved Italian mirror reflects the entire room.

ONE OF MY BIGGEST DILEMMAS—
and everyone should be so lucky!—is that I love so many styles of furniture and decorative objects. I am as fond of Renaissance paintings as modernist chandeliers. I love Swedish painted bureaus as much as English gilt mirrors. And for whatever happy reason, I am especially drawn to odd and eccentric things such as an elephant made of tole or a gnarled Chinese wood stool .

I am an insatiable collector, but I don't consider myself a connoisseur. I know a little about a lot of periods and styles, but I don't have the academic training that is necessary to qualify as an expert. My lack of knowledge sets me free: I blithely mix pieces of varying quality and provenance, creating interesting combinations and unexpected juxtapositions, which has become a hallmark of my design work. Designing a pure 1950s or 1890s interior is a more scholarly approach, but I prefer to put together an assortment of special pieces so that you cannot pigeonhole a room as having a particular "look." Rooms that stand the test of time exude a unique personal style instead of reflecting a specific era or trend.

My tastes are unabashedly eclectic. I can get as excited by an early English oak joined stool as a French eighteenth-century boulle cabinet. A sleek sharkskin-covered table by Jean-Michel

I like to mix painted and stained furniture. The combination of painted Swedish chairs and an English eighteenth-century mahogany table is especially dynamic when paired with a modern painting.

Frank is as beautiful to me as an ornate, carved mahogany one from Portugal. I can just as easily fall in love with a simple Windsor chair as a sophisticated brass inlaid mahogany Russian armchair. And please don't ask me to choose between an intricate Japanese basket and ormolu clock. I look for the integrity of a design, the quality of the craftsmanship, the precision of the finish (or a faded patina), which give a piece of furniture its soul.

I have shopped for furniture all over the world, and I am always searching for unique design and character, wonderful hand finishes, beautiful workmanship, amazing woods—anything that makes a piece distinctive and holds my attention. When working on a project, I photograph pieces that catch my eye, return to my office and lay them out on a table, and start thinking of how to make furniture arrangements and combinations. It becomes a giant puzzle. Once I make a few decisions, then the other pieces have to work perfectly. For a Palladian-style house in Indiana, we found a wonderful set of fourteen nineteenth-century Portuguese dining chairs of intricately carved mahogany. The challenge was finding a table that would do these chairs justice and work in the large, elegant room with its octagon-patterned, coffered ceiling and eighteenth-century Italian onyx mantel. I thought the table should be simple to contrast with the polished wood chairs. So, I designed a very modern table with an angular top of matching rosewood veneers in a striped pattern, which sits on simple rectangular pedestals. The table complemented the other strong pieces I was using: an eighteenth-century painted Italian credenza and a pair of simple hammered metal console tables. All these pieces worked together not because they were alike but because they were different. I like to compare a beautiful room to a great symphony where very different types of instruments—woodwinds, strings, percussion, and brass—come together to create a rich, textured, lyrical sound.

When I begin mixing furniture, I think of the expression "opposites attract," and how I like rooms to combine the masculine and the feminine, the eccentric and the classic, the exuberant and the refined. Think of painted or lacquered chairs around a polished wood table. Think of something sleek against something coarse, something very old with something brand new, something shiny next to something matte. If I have a very ornate mirror, I might want to hang it over a simple table.

I believe in diversity. A room filled with furniture all made from the same wood will be dull, and the pieces will tend to blur together. I don't like rooms filled with only modern furniture for the same reason. But add one rustic object and suddenly the modern pieces will take on a new personality. I have never liked suites of furniture for this reason, and it seems they are finally losing favor with furniture manufacturers and store buyers.

Chairs are probably my favorite type of furniture. They are certainly the best and most interesting way to chart furniture design over the centuries. The nice thing about chairs is that you can have a wide variety of them in your home—comfortable ones for lounging and reading, and character chairs to complete a furniture group for conversation, or to put in a hallway or next to a tub. For every project I always try to find a few chairs with interesting lines that I can float in the middle of a room along with the upholstered pieces. You must always look at chairs from all angles. After all, if your seating group is in the middle of the room, the profile of the chair is very important. And in dining rooms, how a chair looks from the back is more important than how it looks from the front.

Enchanting rooms, like fascinating people, are multidimensional. Just as you can love both football and opera, you can like worn leather chairs and gilded Regency tables. If you accept the idea that many different tastes can go together, you can create rooms that are never boring and always captivating.

A pine-paneled room is filled with an engaging mix: modern metal bookcases, an English Regency desk, a Moroccan rug, and French chairs. The painting is by Manolo Valdes.

A large living room with a nineteenth-century Oushak carpet is furnished with a combination of wood and painted pieces. An Austrian mahogany side chair sits next to a nineteenth-century burl-and-ebonized table. A pair of Louis XVI bergeres are covered in Fortuny fabric.

ABOVE: A Chinese porcelain lamp illuminates a charcoal drawing hung beside a painted Italian chair. RIGHT: An English writing table is perpendicular to a sofa that is paired with a modern Chinese coffee table. A French fruitwood chair sits on a painted sisal rug.

ABOVE: An unusual English Arts and Crafts table with a leather top and nailhead trim is placed next to a sofa upholstered in a bold woven fabric that sits on a French Aubusson carpet. RIGHT: An Irish mahogany console table holds a collection of marble objects. A 1950s drawing of a tiger hangs on deep peach-colored plaster walls.

ABOVE LEFT: In a sitting room, a round painted French table is paired with a painted screen that is set behind the sofa. ABOVE RIGHT: The shape and color of this green lacquer table add interest to a living room. RIGHT: A rare collection of architectural drawings hangs above an eighteenth-century Italian painted credenza. A mixture of wood and lacquer pieces makes for a stimulating, but comfortable, seating group.

The seating group of this living room has a pair of painted French bergeres, an Italian mahogany shell-backed chair, and a pair of modern upholstered chairs grouped around a needlepoint ottoman. The painting is by Robert De Niro Sr.

110

ABOVE: A pool house is furnished with a pair of Deco armchairs and modern metal benches around an Anglo Indian coffee table. A large painted mirror hangs over the sofa.
RIGHT: An eighteenth-century painting of birds hangs over a special French shaped-back sofa with a pair of unusually shaped French wing chairs on each side. Painted carved plaques of fruit and birds from England hang on the wall along with Delft plates.

ABOVE: A breakfast room is furnished with a combination of furniture in different materials. A white painted French cabinet holds a collection of English creamware. The 1950s metal swivel chairs are placed around a French fruitwood table. RIGHT: A set of unusual metal rope chairs surround a stone table that is covered in a printed cotton cloth and set for luncheon on a terrace in Provence.

ABOVE: *A traditional Arabic-style stair railing and contemporary art make for a graphic hallway.* RIGHT: *A modern, hand-hammered four-poster bed with a Greek key border contrasts with the antique wooden beams in this bedroom.*

A rare mahogany French campaign bench sits at the foot of a Victorian tufted leather bed in a room with wool walls. As a contrast, I chose modern metal bedside tables and bookcases, which make each piece more distinct.

VI.
COLOR

A blue-and-white linen carpet and blue and beige fabrics make a strong but simple setting for a Pop Art painting by Roy Lichtenstein. Mellow fruitwood chairs and tables from Italy and France add warmth.

COLOR IS ESSENTIAL TO MY LIFE. I THINK about color all the time. It expresses emotions and evokes memories. When I am driving from the city to the country in the spring, I focus on the pale, delicate greens of trees just beginning to blossom and the soft light that filters through transparent, chartreuse leaves. In the fall, I am mesmerized by the amazingly deep reds, yellows, and ochers. A day doesn't go by that I don't take notice of color. When I go to art galleries and museums, I am always inspired. The other day, for instance, I was looking at a portrait of a lady by Modigliani, and I was struck by the juxtaposition of the periwinkle blue background and the chocolate brown dress she was wearing and thought to myself that I should use that color combination for a room very soon.

I have a wonderful memory for color. I attribute that to my days as an art student when I was taught to mix paints, and learned that colors are actually combinations of colors. I never see colors as one-dimensional. I see a blue-green or a yellow-green, a pinky-red or a purply-red. If you are really interested in color and decorating, I suggest that you buy a simple box of acrylic paints and try mixing your own colors. You will be amazed at how this will open your eyes. You will see how raw umber can soften a color. You will figure out how to tint colors and lighten tones. You will develop a color memory because you will be able to intellectualize the makeup of a color.

Choosing colors is fun, but using them well requires discipline. Most people know what colors they like and dislike. They have strong opinions, especially about colors like purple and orange. Sometimes, a client will say to me, "I hate green," and I will think, *How can you hate green?* Obviously, I wouldn't design a green room for her, but usually a little bit of green will creep in anyway. It's amazing how much color sneaks into a room after

Turquoise Venetian plaster walls complement this dining room's strong architectural elements—Gothic windows and a wooden coffered ceiling. The chairs are upholstered in a rosy red damask. A fanciful crystal chandelier adds sparkle to the room.

you've chosen paint and fabrics. Books, artwork, and flowers all have an impact. If clients have trouble expressing their color preferences, I often ask to see their closets. I can usually learn a lot about their taste from their wardrobes.

I like to have fun with color. I adore the contrast of bright colors with murky colors. One of my favorite colors is a mossy, olivey green. It looks good with turquoise. It looks good with chromium yellow. It looks good with orange. It looks good with almost anything—except other murky colors. It works like a neutral for me, allowing me to play around with stronger, sharper colors (shocking pink, apple green) in supporting roles. That's why I love beiges, but not the ones that are chilly and aloof. My beiges are warm—the color of café au lait, the color of honey. These are neutrals that you can build upon.

White, however, is not a neutral. Frankly, the hardest thing to do is a white room. There are more shades of white than anything in the whole world. And to get harmony with white is almost impossible. You have to be consistent and have all warm whites or gray whites or creamy whites. Every element must be in the same family or that gray white is going to look decidedly more gray than white.

You don't have to be as careful with other colors. Matching everything is not a necessity. If you are working with reds, for example, they don't have to match perfectly, but they need to blend. They need to be in the same family—all orangey reds, pink reds, or violet reds. The goal is harmony and, as with music, there are many ways to achieve that effect. If you put a shocking pink chair in a room, it may be all that you see when you walk in if there are no other pink elements. But if that color is repeated in the room (in welting, pillows, or trim) there will be a sense of unity. Even when you have disparate elements there can be a sense of equilibrium.

To create balance throughout the house, it is essential that at least one color connects each room to the next. If you have a yellow room next to a red room, you must put something yellow in that red room. Houses need to have flow. Otherwise, you end up with a disconcerting jumble. It's very unsettling if there's nothing to link spaces. This is why I often design hallways last. If I have done a number of bedrooms with different color schemes, I try to make the hallway neutral so that it provides a sense of coherence.

I think it is important to choose colors that are easy to live with, which means ignoring trends (which can be difficult when magazines and retailers all push the same hues at the same time). I have been through a lot of decorating eras and everything fashionable eventually becomes passé: quiet, pale rooms, bright Pop Art–inspired rooms, all-beige or all-white rooms. What's timeless is to invent your own color schemes. But I confess that I frequently get the best ideas from looking at antique rugs, which incorporate colors in often unique ways.

When choosing colors, the most important thing to consider is the light. The light in northwestern Connecticut where I spend weekends is different than the light in Dallas or Palm Beach. The light in England is different than the light in the United States. Light affects color drastically. I cannot tell you how many times I've looked at the "perfect" color in my New York office and taken it to a job site only to discover that it is all wrong. New York has very gray light that affects your perception of color. It's also important to consider how a color looks with natural light during the day and with lamp light at night. What I like best are colors that take on a different character depending on the light. For instance, the walls of my living room in Connecticut are an uplifting, sunny yellow during the day but at night they become an apricoty, melon color. The room is moodier in the evening.

The colors in your rooms need to connect to the view outside your window, whether you are in the city or the country. (If you have a room without views, you can pretty much do whatever you want but, funnily enough, the best solution for dark rooms is to keep them dark. If you try to make them light and bright, the effect can be strained and artificial.) I remember an apartment I was decorating in New York that had an entire wall of windows overlooking the East River. Another decorator had used traditional rose-covered English chintz for the walls and curtains, which distracted you from the breathtaking view. It was a total disconnect. One day I was shopping for fabrics at the D & D Building and I found a toile that was exactly right for this room. It had a brown design on top of a pale aqua/sky blue background. I showed a sample to the client and told her it was ideal since it was the same color as the water and the sky. She did not like it at all, and I had to beg her to take it home and see how it looked by her windows. She called me the next day and said, "You are absolutely right. It's perfect." We used the fabric and the effect was quietly spectacular. It's counterintuitive, but gray is a wonderful color for New York apartments. I did a gray wash on the walls of one apartment because it had large windows looking up Fifth Avenue, and I wanted the view to be the focal point of the room.

I t's hard to go wrong when you try to bring the outdoors in. I had clients in the South of France who were very unhappy with their house, which had been decorated in urbane grays and other restrained colors. I went to visit them and was awed by the region's terra-cotta mountains, lavender fields, and golden sunshine. These elements dictated the palette I chose for their house—the same colors that influenced the great Impressionists. Similarly, whenever I work in Aspen or another ski resort out west, I am inspired by the fir trees and evergreens. I want to use rich, enveloping colors that relate to the forests. And for my house in the Dominican Republic, which overlooks the beach, I've used colors that I would never have in my New York apartment, such as sand and bright aqua. In the living room, everything is slip-covered in a pale oceanic blue and the walls are a natural, hand-troweled plaster. For accent colors, I rely on big leaves from the garden and tropical flowers. We even painted one bedroom the exact same lavender as the glorious thunbergia vine that grows on our property. My husband, John, could not believe that I would seriously want to paint a room that color. It seemed, well, out of character for us. But it was so appropriate for the house, and,

rendered in Venetian plaster, it became a complex color that even John could love. Now, it is one of our favorite rooms in the house.

Getting the color right on the walls has become increasingly difficult. When I began my career, we always mixed our own paints. We didn't use a paint chart. I'd come in with a swatch or an idea, and we would mix and make samples on the wall. Today, most painters do not know how to mix. They go by a paint company number. I am glad to see that the paint companies are now selling little jars so you can sample colors before making a commitment. You have to look at paint colors at different times of the day (and remember color looks darker on ceilings than on walls.) I now travel to job sites prepared with my own burnt umber and raw sienna so we can make a color adjustment on the spot. By mixing tints with white paint, we can create what we need and then go back to the paint store and have them match it.

The best commercial paints on the market today are those by Donald Kaufman and Farrow & Ball because they have a richness of color that adds dimension to walls. My favorite way to bring wonderful colors into a house is to have the walls glazed: You have a thin wash of color painted on top of a lighter version of that color. It's similar to the effect you get when painting with watercolors, and it adds depth and character to Sheetrock walls.

Naturally, my passion for color and gardening are inextricably linked, and I am always thinking about what fresh flowers will go in any room. At my house in Connecticut, I have the luxury of planting a cutting garden, and I make sure to grow flowers that will look good in my rooms. I may plant purple flowers in my parterre garden adjacent to the conservatory, but I don't grow them in my cutting garden because they would not look right inside. I grow dark red dahlias for my library and wonderful apricot and peach flowers for the front hall. And though I love yellow flowers, I would never have them in my silver and blue bedroom in New York, where the only blooms that look good are white.

In many ways, colors are like people: They are at their best when they are in relationships with sympathetic souls.

The contemporary art and antique Oushak rug set the tone for this room, which is a blend of warm golden colors and painted and wood French furniture.

126

The color palette for this dining room filled with blue-and-white Chinese porcelains was inspired by the eighteenth-century Chinese wallpaper panels, which hang on natural plaster-finished walls. The chairs are slip-covered in a blue-and-white cotton check.

*ABOVE: The blue-and-white striped sofa fabric combined with a blue pais-
ley print adds a cool contrast to polished butternut paneled walls.
RIGHT: Polished cypress makes for a mellow paneled room, where the blues
and beige in an antique dhurrie rug are repeated in the upholstery.*

The warm rosy red on the sofas can also be found in the French Aubusson carpet. A French printed cotton fabric covers a pair of French fauteuils. Pale blue-gray curtains are a cool counterpoint.

ABOVE: *A bold red silk was used for the walls of this dining room, which has red-and-beige striped silk curtains. The color scheme is repeated on the table, which is set with red Bavarian glass and English, red-bordered botanical china. RIGHT: The walls of this Georgian house were glazed a soft melon color with highlighted trim. The floral chintz used on the chair combines the colors of the walls and the red leather desktop.*

ABOVE: For this living room, the color scheme came from a nineteenth-century English Axminster carpet. The vibrant reds were used as accent colors and appear in the room beyond. RIGHT: The library adjacent to the living room above was painted a shiny red lacquer. The repetition of colors visually links the very different spaces.

A neutral but nevertheless interesting color scheme is accomplished by using a gray-green on the walls and shades of blue and brown for fabrics and the Tibetan rug. A painting by Brice Marden hangs over the French limestone mantel.

ABOVE: *The paneled walls were painted a faded French green to be a backdrop for antique French white painted furniture. RIGHT: The walls of this paneled room were painted in shades of gray as a contrast to the gilded and painted French furniture. The parquet floor is covered with two Aubusson carpets.*

For my own bedroom in New York City, I chose a French blue strie fabric for the walls, which are a refreshing setting for a mirrored canopy bed made by Serge Roche in Paris in the 1940s. The head-board fabric was embroidered in India.

ABOVE: Creams and beiges combine to create a warm living room with French furniture and a bleached floor that was rubbed with white paint. RIGHT: The adjacent entrance hall was painted a rich melon color to counterbalance the graphic black-and-white marble floors.

For a room with natural plaster walls and an antique beamed ceiling, I chose a strong colorful plaid rug. Ochre painted Windsor chairs surround a French country table.

146

VII.
FABRICS

The same delicate French floral cotton is used for the walls, curtains, and upholstery. A bolder fabric with some of the same colors is used for the bed hangings. Antique needlework chairs and textiles contribute to the cozy ambience. The painted chest and mirror are eighteenth-century Italian.

NE OF THE BEST THINGS ABOUT GOING TO WORK

at Parish-Hadley in the 1960s was its proximity to the East 69th Street townhouse of Elinor Merrell, who was New York's leading dealer in textiles. Miss Merrell was a legend. Her five-story townhouse was overflowing with thousands of antique, hand-blocked polished English chintzes, silk Ikat coats from Turkey, embroideries from Uzbekistan, hand-blocked prints from India, *toile de jouy* panels from France, American patchwork quilts, tree-of-life panels from India, and needlepoints from all over the world. Piles of Persian shawls would be stacked next to hand-painted, shimmering silk panels from France.

Miss Merrell became my teacher and my friend. She enlightened, educated, and encouraged me. Her breadth of knowledge was staggering. She was an advisor to curators at Colonial Williamsburg and the Metropolitan Museum of Art, and she helped Mr. du Pont build his great textile collection at Winterthur. She was a force in the New York design world and a founder of the prestigious Winter Antiques Show. She indulged my curiosity and cultivated my nascent passion for textiles. Under her tutelage, I started collecting antique fabrics without knowing exactly what I would do with them, which is still my practice today. At thrift shops, antique shows, and flea markets, I buy material, fold it up, and put it away to use one day on a pillow or a bench. I always like to use at least one antique fabric in every room to add patina. I don't like it when everything is brand-spanking-new. Even when I don't use these beautiful odds and ends, they often provide inspiration for color schemes and other designs.

In the early years of my career, you could buy enough antique fabric to make curtains for an entire room at Miss Merrell's. I might find twenty panels of hand-blocked English glazed chintz already made up as curtains. I

The small-patterned velvet on the chair plays off the striped cotton curtains. A special antique textile lies on the back of the chair to add a grace note and patina.

would have to re-pleat the heading to make them fit a client's windows, but they'd provide instant pedigree for a newly decorated room. You don't come across treasure troves like that anymore.

I wish I could re-create Miss Merrell's magical world. I think the Fabric Room in my office is the next best thing. It's where we work out fabrics schemes, and there is one wall of floor-to-ceiling cubbies filled with fabrics all sorted by color—every shade of blue, every shade of orange, every shade of red has its own bin. I can choose from natural fabrics—linens, cottons, wools, cotton chenilles, cashmeres, silks—in every hue. I find it very distracting to look for fabrics in showrooms because there is so much that I would never use. Whenever I find an appealing fabric, I get a sample for my office collection without necessarily knowing when or where I might use it. Thus, all those hundreds of fabrics in my office are ones that I already *know* I like.

When I start to choose fabrics for a room after settling on a color palette, I focus on mixing textures, solids, and patterns. I often choose a monochromatic fabric for a large sofa, which lets it become a canvas for layering on leopard print throws, needlework pillows, and other patterned items. When I have assembled all the fabrics I want to use for a room, I make a pile of them. If one jumps out, I eliminate it. I want all the fabrics to harmonize. The juxtaposition of the different materials creates a wonderful dynamic. There's nothing better than placing a rugged leather-topped bench next to a genteel linen sofa. My Connecticut living room is a perfect example of my modus operandi: In one room I have furniture covered in a camel-colored silk herringbone weave, a brown linen printed with flowers, a faded cotton toile, a nubby dirty-green chenille, an earthy suede, and antique needlepoint. I am always shopping for

textiles and and adding to my collection. When money is no object, I choose fabrics by Robert Kime, Rose Tarlow, Elizabeth Eakins, and AM Collections, which still offer hand-screened printed fabrics. The softness of a hand-printed fabric is incomparable. I also adore fabrics by Zoffany and Rogers & Goffigon. And Peter Dunham, John Robshaw, Michael Smith, and Kathryn Ireland all have collections that I come back to time after time.

But I also go to places like Pier 1 Imports and Anthropologie to buy batik bedspreads and then cut them up to make pillows or wrap them around sofa cushions so the dogs can lounge. It's one of my oldest tricks and proves that necessity is the mother of invention. Many years ago I fell in love with hand-blocked Indian fabrics but I could not find any place that sold them by the yard. But you could buy Indian bedspreads, which I then started using as tablecloths. And then I thought, *Wouldn't this fabric be great on a pair of English chairs in my front hall?* I still think it's fun to recycle fabrics in unexpected ways. In fact, the brown-and-white toile curtains in my hall were once a pair of bedspreads.

It's very important that fabrics are suitable for how they will be used. If you make silk curtains for a room that gets direct sunlight, you must do something to protect them or the curtains won't last two years. The sun will absolutely rot the silk unless you have solar shades beneath them to screen the light. If you use a strong color on curtains in Florida, it will fade no matter what the material. You have to choose the right fabric for the application. You don't want to choose a heavy, bulky material for the curtains because they won't hang well. You want to make sure the fabric drapes, and that it has what is called a "nice hand."

It's instructive to study how antique chairs and sofas were covered and detailed; it's a good way to learn about the intricacies of upholstery. You'll see the relationship between

A nineteenth-century canopy bed is hung with an original French cotton print. The striped cotton curtains and antique quilt incorporate the same colors, which creates harmony in a room with many different patterns.

the weight of the fabric and the scale of the frame. It's interesting to make a classic French chair contemporary by putting a modern fabric on it. You can be innovative without being outrageous. I once took an eighteenth-century French-style bergere and covered it with a white fabric that I had stitched with black Matisse-inspired squiggles. The abstract design looked fabulous and appropriate on the period chair.

When I am going for a casual, relaxed look, I tend to use slipcovers. They are, of course, very practical, too. If you have a sofa that will be used a lot and will need to be cleaned often, it's great to use a slipcover. I've even upholstered a sofa in a fabric and then made a slipcover in the exact same material so the slipcover can be sent out to be cleaned and the sofa still looks nice.

For the living room of my house in the Dominican Republic, every sofa and chair is slipcovered in the exact same blue cotton duck. It took me forever to find the perfect blue, which is the color of the Caribbean sea. Then I was able to layer the room with pillows made from faded pastel batik sarongs and embroidered Suzani panels from Uzbekistan. It's a lively, energetic room even though all the furniture is covered in a plain fabric. (One big mistake people make when they start decorating is to use boldly patterned fabrics because they have nothing else, but over time the patterns become wearisome and overbearing.)

Finding the right blue fabric was so difficult that I bought enough so that I could make a second set of slipcovers one day. I also reasoned that some pieces would wear out quicker than others and would need to be replaced, so I wanted extra yardage so everything would always match. Of course, the original slipcovers will probably fade and then when I put on the new ones they won't match exactly anyway!

Matching colors, however, is highly overrated. When every thread

A floral chintz corresponds to the colors of the geometric Aubusson-style carpet in a sitting room. The walls were painted in a melon strie and pillows were made from paisley silk and Fortuny fabrics.

in a room coordinates, the feeling is artificial. It's better to have tonal variations of the same color, which is more relaxing than the stiffness of a perfectly calculated palette. The worst thing you can do is pick out colors from your paintings and choose fabrics to match. It belittles the artwork. You want the colors on your furniture to be neutral or a softer version of the colors in your pictures.

You have to be practical with fabrics. There is a suitability factor. If you are doing a sofa where you will be lounging and watching movies, you need something soft, strong, and easy to clean. If you have a chair that is rarely used, then you can use a more fragile material. With three dogs who have the run of the roost, I would never use silk taffeta in my home, though I love it. I use cottons and linens because they are more dog friendly. I often put faux leopard throws on the furniture for my dogs and then never take them off. It's a good look and much nicer than covering a chair with a sheet (or, God forbid, plastic!).

It may sound like I shy away from bold patterns, but that is not accurate. When I use patterned fabrics, I go all out. I might do a bedroom's walls and curtains in one fabric the way the French used toile in the nineteenth century. I love using pattern that way— it makes me think of those amazing paintings of interiors by Bonnard, Vuillard, and Matisse. When you mix several patterns, you must change the scale of them, so if you have a large-scale pattern, you put a thin stripe or tiny check with it. It is very hard to put four very strong patterns in a room. What's more, you need to have a really good upholsterer when you are working with patterned fabrics. She has to know how to match up all the seams and the back and the arms. A bad upholsterer won't even notice, but you will and the results will be disheartening.

For the ultimate in cozy luxury, I will use cashmere for curtains and walls. For elegance, nothing compares to hand-blocked Fortuny. It's hard to print, it takes forever to get, but the results are incomparable. I did the living room of an Italian-style house in Florida with the most incredible green and antique gold Fortuny fabric on the walls. The room had a stone fireplace and a wooden ceiling, and at night with candlelight, the effect was enchanting.

There's nothing better than covering walls with fabric—as long as it's properly done. You can have the fabric upholstered on the walls, which will make the room quiet, or paper-backed and pasted on like wallpaper. If you are working with a nice thin silk, you can have the walls upholstered in knife pleats, which is extremely complicated but breathtaking. Fabrics are one of the many reasons I never tire of my work. They provide an unlimited source of possibilities and pleasures.

A bright pink strie all-weather canvas was used for the cushions on dark metal furniture on a tropical loggia. The throw pillows were made from Indonesian batik fabric.

ABOVE: *An English four-poster bed was hung with Indian embroidered linen. A quilted chintz with similar colors covers a chair and ottoman. The curtains are made from a yellow-and-cream linen print. RIGHT: The pillowcases were embroidered to pick up the golden yellow from the French cotton print used for the bed hangings.*

ABOVE: An American octagon hooked rug covers the floor of this sitting room. An English floral chintz was used for the curtains, a French striped printed cotton on the chair picks up the blue of the rug, and a solid pink linen covers the English sofa. RIGHT: The peaches and blues in the hooked rug set the color palette. The bed curtains are a solid peach lined in blue. The curtains are a floral print incorporating these colors.

LEFT: *The color scheme for this bedroom began with the embroidered felt wall hanging. The bed skirt is a French cotton print that looks smart next to the floral carpet with similar colors.*
ABOVE: *Antique crewel curtain panels were upholstered onto the wall and painted frames were added to the edges. A chair with its original needlework sits on the painted French tile floor.*

Red was the starting point for these two very different bedrooms. *ABOVE: A red plaid silk was decorated with scalloped ribbons for an English four-poster bed. The curtains were made from a French floral print. RIGHT: A red French toile fabric covers the walls and was used for the matching curtains. An American patchwork quilt covers the bed.*

VIII.
KITCHENS AND BATHROOMS

Classic white-painted, raised-panel cabinets with glass doors give a butler's pantry a timeless quality. The room is furnished with a Tibetan rug, an English breakfast table, and handmade South Carolina baskets that hang on the wall.

MOST FAMILIES TODAY LIVE IN THEIR kitchens, not in their living rooms, so I tend to create kitchens that have the same level of design and sophistication as the rest of the house. As with any other room, the floor plan comes first. You've got to get the working area right. The stove, sink, refrigerator, and counterspace for meal preparation should all be near each other so the cook does not have to take too many steps. I find that a counter with an island opposite is the best configuration. When cooking, I want the spices, oils, and utensils I need close at hand, but for the storage of staples, canned goods, and extra paper goods, I love walk-in pantries. At our house in Connecticut, I turned a closet into a walk-in pantry with open shelves so I can see everything I need at once—food magazines, cookbooks, pastas, crackers, popcorn, etc., on one side, and everyday china on the other. On the deep, lower shelves, I store stockpots, trays, and other overscale items. I find this so much more convenient than having to open many small cabinet doors to find the right pan. It is much easier to find what you need when you can scan everything all at once. The same applies to the storage of china and glassware. I prefer narrow cabinets about twelve inches deep so things don't become hidden behind other things, and I can see at a glance all my options for setting a table.

I favor kitchens that have the same decorative and architectural spirit as the rest of the house. I tend to be conservative when it comes to cabinets: White-painted wooden ones are classic, and one never tires of them. They can be painted gray or café au lait for variation, but a neutral kitchen is timeless. A light kitchen also makes a small

To achieve this iridescent blue, I had several layers of different blue paint
applied to these cabinets, which were lightly sanded after each coat.
The countertops are granite and the floors are antique French terra-cotta tiles.

kitchen seem larger. If you choose stained wood cabinets, then the cabinets must be made of high-quality wood such as oak, mahogany, butternut, or cherry, which all look good with a highly polished finish. But I would rather have plain painted white cabinets than badly stained ones made of inferior wood.

Granite countertops are popular for a good reason: They do not stain, and they are heat resistant. I also like sealed limestone, which makes for a mellow countertop in a more rustic kitchen but, alas, can stain. (I always think the first stain is the worst, but eventually, after years of use, limestone counters take on a wonderful patina.) Carrera marble has been used in kitchens for centuries, and it makes an ideal neutral countertop. I always choose a honed finish that is not too shiny. Green or gray soapstones make wonderful countertops too, and I think green marble is snappy with either stained or painted cabinets.

I like a contrast between cabinets and counters, so with dark wood cabinets I will choose a lighter stone; I think dark counters are a really smart counterpoint to light cabinets. I'll often use more than one material for countertops. In areas that are not near a sink, I like to use wood countertops, especially by the cabinets where glass and china are stored since you are less likely to chip your porcelain and crystal on wood than on stone, which is much harder. I would never put stone counters in a butler's pantry.

The backsplash can be an opportunity for more personal expression, but I don't encourage it. The cleanest and most modern look is to use the same material on the counters and backsplash. In a traditional kitchen, tiles can be used, but I firmly believe that you should choose tiles that you are sure will not grow tiresome. As with other rooms in the house, I like to create a neutral backdrop and add color and texture with flowers, artwork, and other decorative objects that can be easily changed to suit your mood or the season.

Kitchen floors are always a problem. Though stone and tile are beautiful, they are uncomfortable to stand on for a long time. They can be noisy and when things fall on them they tend to shatter. (Have you ever noticed that professional kitchens always have thick rubber mats underfoot?) When tile floors seem the best solution, I often add area rugs to soften the space. My favorite kitchen floors are wood—they're warm and easy to stand on for long periods of time. Wood floors can also be painted or stenciled, which can lighten a room and give it added character. I have also found a wonderful vinyl flooring by Amtico that looks like real wood planks; I used it for the kitchen floor in my New York apartment, and no one who visits can believe it's actually vinyl!

As for appliances, it's a decision that's similar to the one you make when buying a car. One person's luxury is another person's necessity. As a homeowner, I think the most important thing is to buy your appliances from a local dealer who can service them. You want someone reliable to call when the dishwasher or refrigerator breaks down on the eve of a big party.

An antique Welsh cabinet provides ample storage in a modern kitchen with an Old World aura. The stove hood is built into a wall that resembles a chimney breast. The vaulted ceiling was painted with vines to simulate an arbor. Terra-cotta tiles cover the floor.

ABOVE: *I used mahogany for the countertops in this butler's pantry because wood is kinder to china and crystal than stone. The glass cabinets are lit from within, and a rolling library ladder makes it easy to reach items stored on the top shelves.* RIGHT: *Hand-painted Portuguese tiles were used for the backsplash in this kitchen with polished marble countertops and polished oak floors.*

ABOVE: In our house in the Dominican Republic, I finally have the pantry of my dreams. Floor to ceiling cabinets with sliding glass doors hold the china sorted by color. The island is fitted with drawers for placemats, napkins, and flatware. Glasses are stored on the upper shelves. RIGHT: Polished butternut cabinets provide handsome storage for china, silver, and linens in this butler's pantry. Antique terra-cotta tiles cover the floor.

*ABOVE: The handsome brass-and-stainless steel hood is connected to the professional-style stove by a metal backsplash. A sculptural stainless pot rack hangs over a wood-topped island. The other counters are black marble, a graphic contrast to the white cabinets.
RIGHT: Ebonized oak cabinets have stainless steel drawer fronts and metal trim on the doors. An antique stone table with a marble top sits on pickled oak floors.*

There is nothing more luxurious than a large bathroom, but not every house can accommodate one. Bathrooms can either be spa-like, with tile or marble walls, or they can feel more like dressing rooms with painted or wallpapered walls. The most important thing to think about in planning any bathroom is storage and lighting. Pedestal sinks may be stylish, but they offer no storage, so you must have a separate closet if you choose them. You also have to think about how the bathroom will function on a daily basis. If the sink area will also be used for doing hair and makeup, then more countertop and storage will be required. In guest bathrooms, it's important to have drawers or cabinets for visitors to put away their toiletries. For smaller, standard-size bathrooms, I prefer white porcelain fixtures and simple white tile around the tub or shower. The walls can then be painted or wallpapered any color. One of my pet peeves is shower curtains. They rarely, if ever, look nice, and they are high maintenance. As long as there is enough space, I always have a separate shower and tub in a bathroom. If you have to have a combination shower/tub, I recommend a rimless glass half door that can be folded back so you don't feel boxed in when bathing.

For floors, I love mosaic tile patterns, which are both practical and special. Painted cement tiles are wonderful and can be done in many patterns and colors. For bathroom floors in places with cold winters, I choose wood floors that can be painted or stained and finished with polyurethane; they are less chilly underfoot.

I am very particular about the installation of tile, because Americans tend to leave too much space for grout. When you see beautiful tiled walls in Portugal or Morocco, the tiles are always set very close together with almost no space for grout. I always insist that tiles be closely set. It can be hard to get workmen to comply, but if you show them a picture of a proper installation, they'll get what you want and why.

When renovating a kitchen or bath or designing a new one, it's important to choose colors, cabinets, tiles, and countertops that you will never tire of. You can always change the colors of the walls with paint or wallpaper. It's much more expensive and exasperating to remove those mauve and orange tiles that you were infatuated with for a brief moment in time.

This stately bathroom designed by architect Jeff Smith is a combination of metal and marble walls and floors. The polished nickel variety and mirror were custom made by L-M-C metal fabricators.

ABOVE: Polished pear-wood walls and cabinets combined with jet black marble make this bathroom sophisticated and sumptuous. Lighting is recessed around the arched satin finished nickel mirror. The Venetian blinds were chosen to match the paneling. RIGHT: This bathroom and dressing room was designed to have generous storage. I hired a decorative painter to embellish the cabinetry with marbleized trompe l'oeil panels. An unusual shell-shaped swivel bench sits at the dressing table.

ABOVE: *A nineteenth-century book of seaweed specimens became the leitmotif for a powder room. They were placed on the wall and molding was added to simulate paneling.* RIGHT: *Embossed leather covers the walls of this powder room, where an antique chest was adapted to hold the sink.*

ABOVE: *A neat-as-a-pin dressing room in bleached mahogany is fitted with a combination of pull-out drawers, shelves, and hanging rods.* RIGHT: *An elegant bathroom with pale glazed paneled walls and gilt trim has an English crystal chandelier hanging over an English eighteenth-century dolphin table. A tufted chair upholstered in terry cloth sits next to the tub. A Victorian slipper chair is placed by the dressing table.*

I used nineteenth-century-style painted cement tiles in turquoise and white and tan and white for these tropical bathrooms. *ABOVE:* A Japanese lacquer corner shelf holds a collection of shells. *RIGHT:* An antique painted canvas screen stands behind the bathtub.

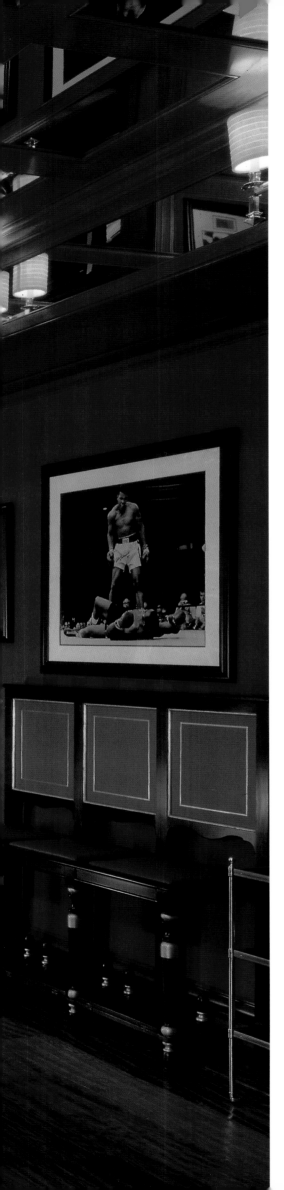

IX.
LIGHTING

The ceiling of this billiard room has mirrored panels illuminated by modern brass light fixtures with parchment shades that were placed around the mahogany soffit. A contemporary billiard fixture with parchment shades is suspended over the antique table. Viewing benches were made for the corners and sides based on antique ones I had seen in a Paris antique shop.

ONE OF THE GOALS OF DECORATING IS TO CREATE

atmosphere, the emotional tone that sets a mood, and nothing effects the mood of a room more than the lighting.

I am amazed at how many times I go into what ought to be a fabulous room where the indifferent and insensitive

lighting plan casts a pall over what would otherwise be magical.

The quantity and quality of light a room needs depends on its uses and the time of day. It is always

important to have light coming from several sources: the ceiling, the walls, and the tables. Certainly, when it

comes to ceiling lights, there can be too much of a good thing. To light a room exclusively with ceiling lights makes

for a harsh, unpleasant experience as they can create a terrible glare. In new houses, there is often a sea of down-

lights pock-marking the ceiling, which creates a Swiss cheese effect. What I find almost universally successful is

placing the ceiling lights in a simple band around the perimeter of the room so the walls are evenly bathed in light.

These lights should be adjustable, and it is best to use ceiling lights that rotate so you do not have light coming

straight down and creating an unpleasant glare. You don't want strong lights overwhelming your seating groups.

If you have a large room with a high ceiling, you can place a chandelier or other hanging light fixture in the

middle of the room with small pin lights on either side.

Wall sconces are a decorative way to bring indirect lighting into a room. You can find beautiful sconces

to complement any style of room. Whether they are modern or traditional, it is important that the lightbulbs

are covered by shades of paper, fabric, or glass. I find looking into bare lightbulbs very unpleasant. Another way

A French eighteenth-century mirror and gilt wood wall sconce brightens
a stone wall. Shirred, off-white pongee shades diffuse the light
from the sconces and the marble column lamps on the side table.

to bring light to the walls is to individually light your paintings with simple picture lights mounted on the frames and focused on the art. I'm a big proponent of lighting bookshelves because otherwise it can be hard to read the spines at night. I like to put small swing arm lamps on the vertical dividers or gooseneck fixtures at the top of the bookcase.

As for lamps, I like to use a variety of shapes and sizes in every room. They are de rigueur next to sofas, beds and between armchairs. If the end tables are a standard 30-inch height, the lamp on that table should be no taller than 28 inches or you will be looking into a lightbulb when you are sitting down. If the tables are lower (say 24 to 26 inches), then taller lamps (36–38 inches) can be used. It is important that the bottom of the shade be lower than eye level when you are sitting in a chair or in bed. This is the rule when installing wall-mounted swing arm lamps next to a bed or sofa, too. I also like small low reading lights with the bulbs covered by a metal or glass shade next to a comfortable chair. They create small pools of light so that reading a book or the newspaper is pleasurable.

Standing lamps can be used when there is not enough room for a table. The height of these lamps if they are being used next to a chair or sofa should be 54 to 60 inches. You can put a taller standing lamp by itself in a corner. For dark corners of a room, torcheres are a good solution. These are lamps that have a bowl-shaped shade with the light focused upwards. The light bounces off the ceiling and provides soft illumination. You can also place uplights on the floor behind a pedestal, plant, or piece of sculpture for a similar but more dramatic effect.

The quality and color of light any lamp provides is dependent on the lampshade. My favorite shades are made from parchment-colored paper, which casts a warm, golden glow. I also like off-white silk pongee shades. If a lamp shade is too white, the light it gives off will be harsh. Sometimes I have custom shades made with a pale pink lining that creates a soft glow that makes every woman in the room look more beautiful. For more drama, dark green or jet black shades in paper or silk are good-looking, but they only emit light from the top and bottom.

It is essential to have all lights on dimmers. If a room is being used for working, the lights can be raised, but they can also be lowered when you are entertaining. Low lights are more atmospheric and cozy. I always put lights on different switches so I can make individual adjustments depending on the occasion and time of day.

Of course, the most beautiful light of all comes from candles. In the dining room, I like to have very soft light from above and many votive candles flickering on the table. I always have hurricanes—candles that have a glass shade around them—all over my house. I have them on the coffee tables, on the mantels, on sideboards, and console tables. I especially like hurricanes with jewel-toned glass. They are atmospheric and magical.

Remember, movie stars often have their own lighting consultants to make sure they always look their best. Your rooms deserve the same star treatment.

Mullioned mirrored doors break up a wall of concealed closets and reflect light from the windows during the day and the lamps at night. The Italian-style bed is draped in printed silk taffeta.

ABOVE: *The lighting in this large living room comes from a gilt wood Italian chandelier hanging over the Portuguese center table and from lamps spaced around the room on various tables.*
RIGHT: *The peaked ceiling of this sun-room is covered in straw matting. A reproduction light fixture based on a design from Kerylos, a Greek villa on the French Riviera, hangs from the center.*

ABOVE: *Adjustable-arm English lights with brass shades illuminate the bookshelves in a pine-paneled sitting room.* RIGHT: *The lighting for this richly paneled mahogany library comes from several sources. Swing arm lamps are mounted on the bookcase, an eight-light Alabaster French chandelier hangs from the ceiling, and a pair of candelabra wired as lamps sits on the desk.*

ABOVE LEFT: For a long hall, parchment and wrought iron fixtures add interest to the ceiling as well as soft light. ABOVE RIGHT: The illusion of skylights was created for this lower-level hall by putting incandescent light behind mullioned frosted glass windows. RIGHT: A row of simple glass bell jars hangs from a vaulted ceiling.

X.
LAYERING

Blue-and-white porcelains in various shapes from several periods are arranged on a side cabinet in front of Chinese wallpaper in a dining room. The antique metal cachepot is handsome even when it's empty but even better when it holds a flowering plant.

O MATTER WHAT THE STYLE OF YOUR HOME,

it is the personal possessions that make your rooms unique and express your personality. Books, paintings, photographs, objets d'art, plants, and bibelots give a room character and bring it to life. Without this aspect of layering, the most exquisitely furnished rooms can have a commercial, anonymous hotel feel. What you choose to display on your tables and shelves and the art that you hang on your walls says so much about who you are.

As I look around my own living room, I am happy to see many things I have collected over the years, which are a constant source of pleasure: the bronze doré clock of a gardener pushing a Versailles tub with a hydrangea plant that I found in a California shop; the bronze of a leaping frog by André Harvey, a wonderful artist and old friend; a pair of wooden planters in the shape of birds that I always admired in Mrs. Parish's apartment that I bought at her estate sale at Sotheby's; the many bronze bunnies by Barré that I've received as gifts from my dear friends Jonathan and Stiles. Every object is meaningful because a story is attached to it. Everything sparks a memory, reminding me of people and places that I treasure.

When you visit me, you know instantly that John and I are bibliophiles because there are books everywhere. You should surround yourself with the things you love, whether they are paintings, porcelains, African masks, or family photographs. If you adore flowers and plants, make the effort to incorporate them into your rooms. When we infuse our spaces with our personality, it reinforces our joie de vivre. What is especially nice about the small

A library with tall, narrow bookcases is furnished with a pair of special rosewood Deco armchairs and a small eighteenth-century French curved back chair, which surround an Anglo Indian coffee table. The juxtaposition of various shapes, sizes, and materials make each piece stand out.

details we add to our homes is that we can move them around and change them, which keeps a house from becoming static and predictable.

I hate clutter, but I love objects as long as they are organized. You must arrange things in a thoughtful manner. I see every tabletop as an opportunity to create a still-life. I can spend hours rearranging objects (such as a collection of porcelain and marble whippets that reflects my husband's passion for his pet whippet, Elizabeth), or creating a "tablescape," as John calls it, that combines a bronze sculpture of a bloodhound, a Wedgwood leaf plate, and an antique terra-cotta pot with a favorite begonia that's in bloom. I love that the leaves of the plant have the same warm, brown color as the patina of the bronze dog.

Every surface is an opportunity for embellishment. The layering and changing of textiles can be great fun. The back of a simple beige sofa can one day have a graphic silk ikat bedspread draped over it with pillows of the same rich colors placed on each side, or the spread could be removed and a faux leopard throw can be folded over the back for a completely different look. A solid, comfortable chair can have a pillow made from an interesting piece of handwoven African fabric to add color and pattern. A room can have all monochromatic pillows and slipcovers in the summer and bright, strong, jewel-colored ones for the dreary winter months.

While it is wonderful to surround oneself with photographs of family and friends, you should do so with careful consideration. I like groups of picture frames when they are all the same—say, silver or parchment-colored wood.

As long as they are the same material and color, they can be different sizes. One or two groupings of photographs is enough for any room; otherwise, they turn into a distracting hodgepodge. I cannot stand walking into a room and seeing little picture frames dotting every surface. One of my favorite ways to incorporate family photographs is to edit them and have the best ones enlarged to at least 18 by 24 inches. I then put them in simple frames and hang them in bedroom halls and along staircases, where they can be enjoyed on a daily basis.

It is always more aesthetically rewarding to put things together when they have something in common. A shelf with a collection of items that relate to each other will make more of a statement than individual, unrelated pieces just placed on a shelf or tabletop to get them out of the way. The groupings can be organized by material, color, or subject matter such as gardening, sailing, or ornithology. Each piece needs to relate in some way to the other ones.

Many people prefer a spare, minimal style, but even then a single eye-catching hand-thrown pottery bowl can do wonders for a simple glass-topped coffee table. You don't need many objects, but they should always have strong character. And no matter what your taste in decorating, you must find places for everyday things—a big basket for the day's newspaper and magazines; a beautiful tray set on a side table made ready for drinks with glasses, ice bucket, corkscrew, small bottles of sodas and mixers; a stack of current books; a special cachepot for a delicate orchid; or a handsome vase filled with fragrant roses. Without layers and small touches, a house never truly becomes a home.

A painted nineteenth-century Provincial French screen hangs behind a country pine table with a marble top.
A pair of alabaster columns were made into lamps. The large screen gives great scale to the long wall.

ABOVE: *Chinese porcelain birds surround a painted wood column lamp. RIGHT: For my New York living room, I combined a Chinese coffee table with Swedish chairs and a modern upholstered sofa copied from a French 1940s design, which is enlivened by needlework pillows in several geometric patterns. Family photographs in silver frames sit beside a Japanese porcelain lamp on a black lacquer English table.*

In this living room, a collection of drawings and mirrors hangs over a long table set with a drinks tray that is always ready for guests. A large seating group that includes a small English sofa and a pair of Directoire chairs is arranged on an unusual Chinese rug. A pair of nearby benches can be pulled up when additional seating is required.

ABOVE: *Marble and metal objets d'art are thoughtfully arranged on a felt-covered end table in a library.* RIGHT: *Unusual wooden pedestals with matching urns are filled with palm trees to accentuate the height of this room. Eighteenth-century French gilt wood chairs flank an unusual English Gothic-style nineteenth-century console table.*

ABOVE: On a trip to California, I found this French ormolu clock that I could not live without. As a gardener, this piece resonated with me. The objects in our homes should always reflect our passions.
RIGHT: This carved twig mirror in my New York living room hangs over the mantel, which holds a pair of painted plaster Turkish figures sitting on cushions. The half-round planters are always filled with fresh flowers or greens.

A client's collection of architectural drawings gives this living room a unique character. The center table holds a welcoming drinks tray so guests can help themselves.

ABOVE: I can never find enough places for books. I designed this black lacquer bookcase for my entrance hall. I like to have fresh flowers on the Irish center table. The herringbone parquet floor is stained three different shades.
RIGHT: There are more books in my library/dining room. A marbleized column holds a Turkish plaster bust. English Regency chairs surround a table covered with an Indian cotton print tablecloth and set for an intimate supper party.

ABOVE: An ancient bronze horse and modern pottery are displayed on top of an Anglo Indian chest.
RIGHT: A Delft garniture set is arrayed on a reproduction French marbleized mantel with early brass
candlesticks balancing on the edges. A seventeenth-century painting of a bird hangs over the fireplace.

LEFT: *A beautiful antique bronze head graces a tabletop. ABOVE: In this library/dining room, an English Arts and Crafts table sits on a custom designed Tibetan rug. A piece of Japanese pottery was wired as a lamp. The nineteenth-century Irish mahogany bookcase holds a collection of rare books.*

XI.
INSPIRATION

The ebony-and-mahogany doors for
this New York apartment were inspired
by ones I saw in St. Petersburg.

NOTHING IS AS ENLIGHTENING AND educational as travel. From my seminal, eye-opening visit at the age of fifteen to the Dorothy Draper–decorated Greenbrier resort in West Virginia to my recent trip to see the newly refurbished Musée des Arts Decoratifs in Paris, I have been continually inspired by visiting houses, gardens, and museums around the world. My idea of a great vacation is to tour the manor houses of England, the palaces of India, the chateaux of France, and the Palladian villas of the Veneto.

Books and magazines fuel my wanderlust. I recently read a new book on Portuguese houses and gardens, which made me want to hop on a plane immediately. After paging through *Neoclassicism in the North: Swedish Furniture and Interiors 1770–1850*, I started planning a trip to Scandinavia. Even when you cannot travel overseas, you can be inspired by photographs, which is why you'll always find stacks of books and magazines in my home.

I owe my interest in how other people live and furnish their homes to my mother. She used to take me to visit the old plantation houses on the James River in Virginia. We'd go on house and garden tours in Charleston and Savannah. The curiosity bug was planted in my brain. Seeing how fine old families arranged their furniture and hung their pictures gave me ideas that I stored away without realizing how useful they would be to me one day.

To hang over the Lutyens fireplace in a dining room, I designed a large verre eglomise sunburst mirror based on one I saw in an English country house. The dining table was inspired by a photograph of a table by the fashionable French firm Jansen that I had clipped from a magazine many years ago.

I don't like to forget good ideas, and for decades I have been cutting pictures out of magazines and pasting them in scrapbooks. On my journeys, I take lots of photographs, but they rarely include my traveling companions. I am usually taking pictures of a floor pattern in a Venetian villa or a mahogany door from a Russian palace. The photograph I took of the light that filtered through an Indian Jolie screen became an idea for a window treatment. The tiled walls of Morocco and Portugal inspired a bathroom at a ranch in Texas and a kitchen in Florida. The painted ceiling in the Sintra Palace in Portugal became the starting point for a kitchen in Connecticut.

When I first went to work in New York for the antiques dealer Stair & Co., I would spend Saturdays going to Sotheby Parke-Bernet and Plaza Art Galleries (which was eventually bought by Christie's) to see what was being sold that week at auction. Poring through auction catalogues is still one of my favorite pastimes. I often buy old catalogues, for they are filled with clear pictures and the essential facts about decorative arts and paintings. If you want to see what's currently for sale, you can subscribe to the auction catalogues. You can also purchase old catalogues, which are just as educational and usually less expensive on the Internet from sources like The Strand.

Visiting museums is a must for anyone interested in design, and the more you go, the more you will train your eye to appreciate things of great quality, which is essential if you are to discover treasures on your shopping trips. You can find a wonderful color scheme, for instance, by studying the Egyptian frescos at the Metropolitan Museum of Art. When I see the paintings of Vuillard, Bonnard, Balthus, and Matisse, I want to re-create the feeling of their intimate, luscious interiors. Looking at fine French furniture, exquisite Japanese lacquer, and early Etruscan pottery is nourishment for the imagination. Studying antique costumes can provide ideas for a curtain trim or an embroidered cushion. If you live near a great museum, take advantage of the lectures that are offered. Search out organizations, such as the Garden Conservancy, that offer tours of private gardens and houses. I will never forget a tour arranged by the Institute of Classical Architecture & Classical America, which afforded me the opportunity to see the great early twentieth-century estates of Chicago's North Shore designed by David Adler.

Over the years, my own library has grown and grown, and there is still nothing I would rather receive than a new book, which I usually devour immediately. I especially love to find a volume on a new furniture designer or a catalogue raisonné of a contemporary architect that inspires me to envision a modern house I might someday design for John and myself. When you are curious and open-minded, you see the world as filled with unlimited opportunities for discovering new people, places, and things.

I found ideas for painting this coffered wood ceiling in my picture collection of Italian houses. French chairs float on a needlepoint rug based on an Aubusson design.

I had the walls of this sitting room painted in panels to simulate rococo plasterwork with brackets I had seen in a Russian summer pavilion outside St. Petersburg. The brackets hold a collection of Delft porcelains.

I have visited Portugal many times and always admire the country's amazing hand-painted tiles. I was excited when I realized I could use hand-painted tiles around the tall arched doors in this breakfast/sitting room as well as for the wainscot.

The Moorish trompe l'oeil marbleized door trim was based
on a Portuguese door frame I saw at the palace in Sintra.
The painted furniture sits on a plaid cotton rug that reminds
me of the one I grew up with in Virginia.

I was inspired by rustic Swiss Alpine houses when designing this room in the Southwest that has limed oak board walls with rough plaster chinking between the planks. Austrian-style wool carpets cover the chestnut floors.

For the custom-painted walls of this dining room in a country house with an amazing garden, I was inspired by a panel of eighteenth-century French canvas wallpaper. French chairs with their original floral needlework surround an English eighteenth-century pedestal table.

ABOVE: Early Azulejos—glazed and painted tiles used for wainscot or facing—set the mood for this Mediterranean house, which has highly polished terra-cotta tile floors with decorative medallions. RIGHT: The ceiling of a Venetian palazzo was the inspiration for this dramatic room. The terrazzo floors were poured to simulate those that cover the houses of the Veneto.

For the domed ceiling of this house designed by
Mark Ferguson, I was inspired by a painted
ceiling from Sir John Soane's Museum in Lon-
don. Chuck Fisher re-created this honeycomb
lattice pattern entwined with honeysuckle.

*A pair of ivory four-poster beds that Francis Elkins designed for
a house in Chicago have resided in my memory for a very long
time. I designed a similar bed in wood and had it painted in faux
ivory. The valance and headboard were embroidered in India.
An antique cotton Indian dhurrie covers the floor.*

XII.
LA COLINA

The front of our house, designed by Ernesto Buch, was inspired by the raised cottages of the American South. You enter by going up one of the two circular staircases to the main living spaces.

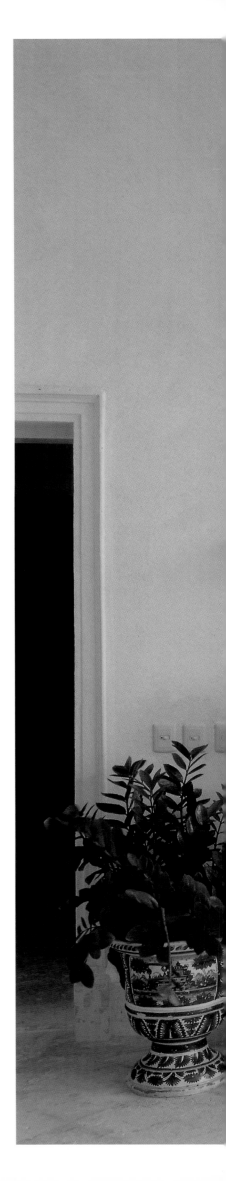

M Y HUSBAND, JOHN ROSSELLI, is my all-time favorite client, but also a very defiant one. He has very strong tastes, yet we have collaborated harmoniously on several major projects at Manor House, our country retreat in northwestern Connecticut, which was chronicled in my book *An Affair with a House.* Until we bought land in the Dominican Republic, however, we had never designed and built a house from the ground up.

Over the years, we often visited our friends Annette and Oscar de la Renta in the Dominican Republic, and we fell in love with Punta Cana, a community that Oscar and his partners have developed. We decided to build our dream house in Punta Cana, overlooking the azure Caribbean sea. Armed with books on the Southern raised cottages that we've always loved, we met with Ernesto Buch, a classical architect whose work we had admired, and started the plan for the house that we call La Colina (The Hill).

Our design called for a living room and long porches on the second floor—the *piano nobile*—to take advantage of the ocean view. We were certain that we wanted a house where we would mostly live and dine outside, so the house was designed with large double porches in both the front and the back. French doors open from each bedroom

On the entrance and dining porch, a mirror made from antique pilasters hangs over a modern console table by Iatesta that holds a collection of blue-and-white porcelain.

onto porches with large chaises perfect for reading in the morning and napping in the afternoon. We have triple-hung windows on the two long sides of the living room, and we can open them so the soft, tropical breeze blows through the room. I have loved triple-hung windows since the very first time I saw them at Thomas Jefferson's Monticello. I had mine made by Zeluck, the venerable window manufacturer, which was another dream come true.

The house consists of four bedrooms, a living room, a kitchen, a television/library/game room, and my favorite room, a large butler's pantry. The pantry has floor-to-ceiling cabinets with sliding glass doors, and they are filled with china and glassware. There is a center island with drawers for storing flatware, napkins, placemats, and other table accessories. The large countertop allows me to plan and experiment with table settings without having to carry them out to one of the porches where we usually have our meals.

Luckily, we already owned most of the furniture. John's former house in New Jersey was filled with wonderful, large-scale pieces and so was his house in Savannah. I had many pieces that I had bought over the years and kept in storage because I could not part with them. I took photographs of all the pieces we owned along with their measurements and, having done the floor plans for each room, assigned each one a new home. Everything was polished, recovered, or slipcovered in off-white duck or in an ocean-blue cotton for the living room. Pieces that had been covered in dark velvets or tapestries in a previous life were now reconceived for the tropics. It was amazing how good all the things we owned and loved look in the new house. We had to buy a few more upholstered chairs and sofas as well as all-weather rattan furniture for the verandas.

As the living room rises fifteen feet to the cornices with a coved ceiling that rises even higher, we feared we did not have enough large-scale pieces. I found two exceptional ten-foot mirrors that we ordered from China, and John painted them a chalky white when they arrived. On either side of the mirrors, I envisioned four large scenic panels; knowing that I would never find four antique ones, I decided to commission them. I wanted paintings of palm trees and white water birds. John was able to find an artist from the stable of talented artisans in his studio, and my vision was carried out even better than I had imagined. The panels are four by eight feet and the frames are painted faux bamboo. All of these large pieces make the room at once more exciting and cozy. When a large room has furniture that is too small, the effect can be unsettling.

My entire approach to the decoration of La Colina was to keep the backgrounds simple and to use what

PREVIOUS PAGE: Tall triple-hung windows by Zeluck line two walls of the living room, creating cross ventilation. The room is furnished with an assortment of pieces that John and I already owned, which we refinished and recovered. The coral stone floors are covered with an Indian cotton dhurrie rug. RIGHT: All of the furniture in the living room was slipcovered in clear, sea-blue cotton. The panel of white birds that hangs above an Irish console was painted by John's studio.

we owned and loved. The bedrooms are each done in a different shade of Venetian plaster: We chose turquoise for our bedroom (a color John always said he hated but in this case he trusted my vision and now loves it). The guest rooms are in tropical-inspired colors: cantaloupe, banana yellow, and a lavender that is the same color as the flowers on the beautiful thunbergia vines that grow outside our windows. The rugs are either sisal or cotton, and the patterns in each room come from the layering of fabrics on chaises and the bedcovers, which I change from time to time.

When John and I were shopping in France for Treillage, the garden antiques shop we own in Manhattan, we spotted the most wonderful pair of Biedermeier sleigh beds. I bought them immediately, and I knew they would be spectacular floating in the center of the yellow bedroom. This arrangement allowed us to hang unobstructed two rare, early nineteenth-century wallpaper panels of ships at sea by Dufour, the great French wallpaper maker, which I had owned for ten years but had never been able to use. I sent them off to be restored by conservator John Nawalla. The combination of the beds and the panels makes for a very special room, especially in the Caribbean.

I have to admit that everything was not always heavenly. At one point, I did tell John that he was the worst client I ever had because he really only has enthusiasm for white walls and sisal, which are his preferred backdrop for his many collections and antiques. But as we respect each other enormously, we found common ground and had an amazing time creating La Colina together. Now the only challenge is finding enough time to enjoy its transcendent magic.

Rattan chairs surround the large stone dining table, which was made for us in France. It is set with large hurricanes that we light every night.

ABOVE: *The interior staircase became the home for the Swedish bird prints and a carved and guilded cartouche, which had been in John's house in Savannah.*
RIGHT: *A large turtle shell that John has owned forever sits on a simple Italian serpentine table with a large Dutch mirror hanging on the wall. The chair in the foreground is nineteenth-century Victorian covered in a leopard print fabric.*

The much-used TV room on the first
floor is furnished with a very long sofa
and comfortable chairs, ready for the
next movie. A game table for cards or a
jigsaw puzzle stands in the corner.

LEFT: I chose vivid turquoise Venetian plaster for the master bedroom walls. The mahogany bed is nineteenth-century American. A richly carved mirror hangs above an English black lacquer chest. ABOVE: The corner of the bedroom has a huge chaise covered in an embroidered Suzanni. A writing table sits in front of a shuttered window.

When we saw these Biedermeier sleigh beds at a fair in Provence, I immediately envisioned them in the center of this guest bedroom, which has Venetian plaster walls tinted bright yellow. A cotton rug covers the stone floor.

ABOVE: *John's bathroom is furnished with an Anglo Indian ebony chair and an English mahogany towel stand. RIGHT: The adjacent dressing room has a French painted daybed and a collection of Indian paintings.*

ABOVE: *The facade of the pool house, which was inspired by a Greek temple, is reflected in the water.* RIGHT: *We read, nap, and gaze at the ocean from the main room of the pool house, which is furnished with comfortable synthetic rattan furniture.*

ABOVE: One of a pair of painted Regency shelves that hold a collection of coral and shells, which hang on either end of the pool house. RIGHT: I had owned these mirrored Venetian doors for years and I was happy to have finally found the perfect spot for them. They hang on either side of an archway that leads to a circular garden. The weathered coffee table is from Thailand.

RESOURCES

ARCHITECTS

Ferguson & Shamamian, 270 Lafayette Street, New York, NY 10012

Jeff Smith, 206 Phipps Plaza, Palm Beach, FL 33480

John B. Murray, 36 W. 25th Street, New York, NY 10010

Nasser Nakib, 145-147 E. 57th Street, New York, NY 10022

Kean Williams Giambertone, 5 Main Street,
  Cold Spring Harbor, NY 11724

Thomas M. Kirchhoff, 1907 Commerce Lane, Jupiter, FL 33458

Hottenroth & Joseph, 152 Madison Avenue, New York, NY 10016

Ernesto Buch, 508 Russell Street, New Haven, CT 06513

David H. Ellison, 6403 Detroit Avenue, Cleveland, OH 44102

Gil Schafer, 270 Lafayette Street, New York, NY 10012

DECORATIVE PAINTERS

Chuck Fisher, 1530 Broadway, New York, NY 10036

Clifton Jaeger, PO Box 5, Falls Village, CT 06031

John Rosselli, 523 E. 73rd Street, New York, NY 10021

Franklin Tartaglione, 8 Old Fulton Street, Brooklyn, NY 11201

De Gournay, 143 West 29th Street, New York, NY 10001

RUGS

Doris Leslie Blau, 306 E. 61st Street, New York, NY 10021

Beauvais, 595 Madison Avenue, New York, NY 10022

F.J. Hakimian, 136 E. 57th Street, New York, NY 10022

Darius, 981 Third Avenue, New York, NY 10022

A.M. Collections, 584 Broadway, New York, NY 10012

Stark Carpet, 979 Third Avenue, New York, NY 10022

Patterson, Flynn & Martin, 979 Third Avenue, New York, NY 10022

Shyam Ahuja, 201 E. 56th Street, New York, NY 10022

Elizabeth Eakins, 21 E. 65th Street, New York, NY 10021

Abadjian, 200 Lexington Avenue, New York, NY 10016

Laura Fisher, 305 E. 61st Street, New York, NY 10021

FABRICS

Robert Kime, Arthur Dunham, Katherine Ireland all available
  at John Rosselli, 979 Third Ave, New York, NY 10022

A.M. Collection, 584 Broadway, New York, NY 10012

Peter Fasano Ltd, 964 South Main Street, Great Barrington, MA 01230

Rogers and Goffigon Ltd, 41 Chestnut Street,
  Greenwich, CT 06830

Claremont, 1059 Third Avenue, New York, NY 10021

Chelsea Textiles, 183 Mill Lane, Mountainside, NJ 07092

FLOORING

William J. Erbe, 560 Barry Street, Bronx, NY 10474

Baba, 4380 Alston Chapel Road, Pittsboro, NC 27312

Janos Spitzer, 131 W. 24th Street, New York, NY 10011

AAA World Floors Inc., P.O. Box 33282,
  Decatur, GA 30033-0282

METAL WORK

LMC, 77 Second Avenue, Patterson, NJ 07514

Schwartz's, PO Box 205 Forge Hollow Road,
  Deansboro, NY 13328

CURTAIN AND CUSTOM UPHOLSTERY

A Schneller, 129 W. 29th Street, New York, NY 10001

De Angelis, 312 E. 95th Street, New York, NY 10128

Milillo Interiors, 207 E. 84th Street, New York, NY 10028

Kay Neal, 1733 School Street, P.O. Box 85,
  Thompson Station, TN 37179

Wainland's, 24-60 47th Street, Astoria, NY 11103

EMBROIDERY

Penn & Fletcher, 21-07 41st Avenue, Long Island City, NY 11101

Holland & Sherry, 979 Third Avenue, New York, NY 10022

PANELING

Froelich, 550-560 Barry Street, Bronx, NY 10474

Merritt Woodwork, 7198 Industrial Park Boulevard,
  Mentor, OH 44060

FINISHING

Laszlo's, 37 W. 26th Street, New York, NY 10010

MUSEUMS

BEAUPORT
(Henry Davis Sleepers House)
75 Eastern Point Boulevard
Gloucester, MA 01930
978-283-0800
www.historicnewengland.org

WINTERTHUR
Route 52
Winterthur, DE 19735
302-888-4600
www.winterthur.org

MONTICELLO
931 Thomas Jefferson Parkway
Charlottesville, VA 22902
434-984-9822
www.monticello.org

MOUNT VERNON
3200 Mount Vernon Memorial Highway
Mount Vernon, VA 22121
703-780-2000
www.mountvernon.org

COLONIAL WILLIAMSBURG FOUNDATION
Colonial Williamsburg, VA 23187
757-220-7234
www.colonialwilliamsburg.com

EDSEL & ELEANOR FORD HOUSE
Grosse Pointe Shores, MI 48236
313-884-4222
www.fordhouse.org

FRANK LLOYD WRIGHT PRESERVATION TRUST
Oak Park, IL 60302
708-848-1976
www.wrightplus.org

HEARST CASTLE PRESERVATION FOUNDATION
San Francisco, CA 94104
415-296-8550
www.hearstcastle.org

HENRY MORRISON FLAGLER MUSEUM
Palm Beach, FL 33480
561-655-2833
www.flaglermuseum.us

HILLWOOD MUSEUM & GARDENS
Washington, DC 20008
202-686-8500
www.hillwoodmuseum.org

ISABELLA STEWART GARDNER MUSEUM
Boston, MA 02115
617-278-5132
www.gardnermuseum.org

PEBBLE HILL FOUNDATION
Thomasville, GA 31799
229-226-2344
www.pebblehill.com

TRYON PALACE HISTORIC SITES AND GARDENS
New Bern, NC 28563
252-514-4900
www.tyronpalace.org

VIZCAYA MUSEUM AND GARDENS
Miami, FL 33129
305-860-8422
www.vizcayamuseum.org

HOMEWOOD HOUSE MUSEUM
Baltimore, MD 21218
410-516-5589
www.museums.jhu.edu/homewood

AIKEN-RHETT HOUSE
Charleston, SC 29401
843-723-1159
www.historiccharleston.org

TOURS BY THE INSTITUTE OF CLASSICAL ARCHITECTURE & CLASSICAL AMERICA
212-730-9646
www.classicist.org

JAMES RIVER PLANTATIONS
House and Garden Tours
804-829-2196
www.jamesriverplantations.org

MY DESIGN LIBRARY

I own thousands of books, but these volumes are especially educational and inspirational. A great resource for new and out-of-print volumes on design is Potterton Books (www.pottertonbooks. co.uk), which has a shop in New York City.

Albert Hadley: The Story of America's Preeminent Interior Designer by Adam Lewis (Rizzoli, 2005)

American Classicist: The Architecture of Philip Trammell Shutze by Elizabeth Meredith Dowling (Rizzoli and Atlanta Historical Society, 1989, reprinted in 2001)

An Ilustrated History of Interior Decoration from Pompeii to Art Nouveau by Mario Praz (Thames and Hudson, 1964, various editions published)

The Best of Elle Déco by Jean Demachy, ed. (Hachette and Filipacchi, 1997)

Billy Baldwin Decorates by Billy Baldwin (Holt Rinehart and Winston, 1972)

Class Act: William Haines Legendary Hollywood Decorator by Peter Schifando and Jean H. Mathison (Pointed Leaf Press, 2005)

Classical European Furniture Design: French, Spanish and English Period Designs, 3 volumes in 1 (Gramercy Publishing, 1989)

Classical Swedish Architecture and Interiors by Johan Cederland (Norton, 2007)

Colefax and Fowler: The Best in Interior Decoration by Chester Jones (Bulfinch, 1997)

Contemporary: Architecture and Interiors of the 1950s by Lesley Jackson (Phaidon Press, 1994, reprinted in paperback)

David Adler Architect: The Elements of Style by Richard Guy Wilson et al. (Yale and University of Chicago, 2002)

Decoration, 4 volumes, by the Staff of *Connaissance des Arts,* Pierre Levailles et al. (English edition, Hachette 1963–68)

Decoration: Tradition et Renouveau by Claude Fregnac (Réalités, 1973)

The Decoration of Houses by Edith Wharton and Odgen Codman, Jr. (Scribner's, 1897, new edition, Rizzoli, 2007)

The Design Encyclopedia by Mel Byars (The Museum of Modern Art, 2004)

The Eight Major Decorating Styles Seen in Today's Most Beautiful Rooms by Minn Hogg, Wendy Harrop, and *The World of Interiors* (Clarkson Potter, 1988)

Elements of Style: An Encyclopedia of Domestic Architectural Detail by Stephen Calloway, Alan Powers, and Elizabeth Cromley (new edition, Firefly Books, 2005)

Elsie de Wolfe: A Decorative Life by Nina Campbell and Caroline Seebohm (Panache Press, 1992)

English Decoration of the 18th Century by John Fowler and John Cernaforth (Barrie and Jenkins, 1974, various editions published)

The Finest Rooms by America's Great Decorators by Katharine Tweed (Viking Press, 1965)

Frances Elkins: Interior Design by Stephen Salny (Norton, 2004)

The French Interior in the Eighteenth Century by John Whitehead (Laurence King, 1992)

The Genius of Robert Adam: His Interiors by Eileen Harris (Yale, 2001)

The Givenchy Style by Françoise Mohrt (Vendome Press, 1998)

Horst Interiors by Barbara Plumb (Bulfinch, 1993)

House & Garden's New Complete Guide to Interior Decoration, fifth edition, by the editors of *House & Garden* (Simon and Schuster, 1953)

The House in Good Taste by Elsie de Wolfe (The Century Co., 1913, reprinted in 2004)

In the Pink: Dorothy Draper America's Most Fabulous Decorator by Carleton Varney (Pointed Leaf Press, 2006)

Jansen: Decoration by Jacques Leveque, ed. (Société d'études et de publications économiques, 1971)

Jean-Michel Frank by Adolphe Chanaux with Leopold Diego Sanchez (reprint edition, Editions du regard, 1997)

Legendary Decorators of the Twentieth Century by Mark Hampton (Doubleday, 1992)

Mark Hampton on Decorating by Mark Hampton (Random House, 1989)

Nancy Lancaster: English Country House Style by Martin Wood (Frances Lincoln, 2005)

New York: Trends and Traditions by Roberto Schezen and Chessy Rayner (Monacelli Press, 1997)

Nineteenth-Century Decoration: The Art of the Interior by Charlotte Gere (Harry N. Abrams, 1989)

On Living—With Taste by David Hicks (Frewin Publishers Ltd, 1968)

Parish Hadley: Sixty Years of American Design by Sister Parish, Albert Hadley, and Christopher Petkanas (Little Brown, 1995)

Roomscapes: The Decorative Architecture of Renzo Mongiardino by Renzo Mongiardino, Fiorenzo Cattaneo, ed. (Rizzoli, 1993)

Sixty Years of Interior Design: The World of McMillen by Erica Brown (Viking Press, 1982)

Syrie Maugham by Richard B. Fisher (Duckworth, 1979)

The Penguin Dictionary of Decorative Arts by John Fleming and Hugh Honour (Viking, 1989)

Twentieth Century Decoration by Stephen Calloway (Rizzoli, 1988)

Vogue's Book of Houses, Gardens, People by Diana Vreeland, Valentine Lawford, and Horst (Viking, 1968)

The Way We Live Now by Stafford Cliff (Clarkson Potter, 2004)

PHOTOGRAPHY CREDITS

Fernando Bengoechea: Pages 128, 148

Anita Calero: Page 23

Tim Clinch: Page 115, 116, 126, 132, 153, 200

Billy Cunningham: Pages 2, 26, 54, 160, 165, 232, 236, 240

Pieter Estersohn: Pages 9, 18, 20, 36, 142, 207, 212, 213, 216, 217

Oberto Gili: Pages 56, 85, 94, 95, 101, 151, 159, 208, 218, 219, 228

Matthew Hranek / A+C Anthology: Pages 67, 123, 195, 239

Michael Mundy: Pages 52, 64, 93, 135

John Vaughan: Pages 105, 144, 145, 206

Fritz von der Schulenburg: Pages 5, 16, 25, 30, 32, 34, 35, 38, 39, 40, 43, 45, 47, 48, 50, 51, 53, 58, 59, 60, 61, 62, 63, 68, 70, 71, 72, 73, 74, 77, 78, 81, 83, 84, 86, 87, 88, 89, 90, 92, 96, 99, 102, 106, 107, 110, 112, 113, 118, 120, 130, 131, 134, 136, 137, 138, 140, 141, 146, 147, 156, 158, 161, 162, 163, 164, 166, 169, 171, 172, 173, 174, 175, 176, 177, 180, 182, 183, 184, 185, 186, 187, 188, 191, 193, 194, 196, 197, 198, 199, 203, 205, 210, 211, 220, 221, 222, 225, 226, 230, 231, 235, 242, 244, 247, 248, 251, 252, 254, 255, 256, 258, 259, 260, 262, 263, 264, 265, 266, 267

Published in 2007 by Stewart, Tabori & Chang
An imprint of Harry N. Abrams, Inc.

Text copyright © 2007 by Bunny Williams and Dan Shaw

All rights reserved. No portion of this book may be reproduced, stored in a retrieval system, or transmitted in any form or by any means, mechanical, electronic, photocopying, recording, or otherwise, without written permission from the publisher.

Library of Congress Cataloging-in-Publication Data:

Williams, Bunny, 1944-
   Bunny Williams' point of view : three decades of decorating elegant and comfortable houses / written with Dan Shaw ; photographs by Fritz Von Der Schulenburg ; book design by Doug Turshen, with David Huang.
     p. cm.
   ISBN-13: 978-1-58479-624-4
   ISBN-10: 1-58479-624-3
1. Interior decorating—Psychological aspects. I. Title.

NK2113.W538 2007
747—dc22   2007008889

Editor: Dervla Kelly
Designer: Doug Turshen with David Huang
Production Manager: Jacquie Poirier

The text of this book was composed in Requiem

Printed and bound in China
10 9 8 7 6 5 4 3

HNA
harry n. abrams, inc.
a subsidiary of La Martinière Groupe

115 West 18th Street
New York, NY 10011
www.hnabooks.com